W9-CMA-628

DEDICATED
to my teacher
FUNAKOSHI GICHIN

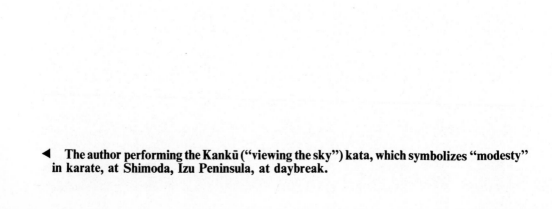

◄ The author performing the Kankū ("viewing the sky") kata, which symbolizes "modesty" in karate, at Shimoda, Izu Peninsula, at daybreak.

Table of Contents

Preface

THIS BOOK is not intended to reveal any secrets of karate, because there are no mysteries involved in the study of this martial art. The purpose of this publication is to provide a textbook for the karate student based on the techniques I have acquired during my more than thirty-year study and teaching of the art. Fundamental techniques and movements have been thoroughly analyzed, categorized, and arranged systematically to serve as a complete guide.

My teacher, Funakoshi Gichin, changed the concept of *karate-jitsu* (literally, "Chinese hand techniques") to *karate-dō* (literally, "empty-hand ways") in 1935, and published the *Karate-dō Kyōhan*. This outstanding book was primarily intended as a character-building source book, but it also explains the spiritual contents of karate, classifies the various techniques, and provides an evaluation of karate as a course of physical education. Feeling the need for a modern and complete manual, I have taken the techniques mentioned in my teacher's book and have spent ten years compiling a new text of fundamental techniques based on my teaching experience at the Japan Karate Association.

Another factor which prompted me to publish this book was the growing popularity of karate as a sport. This development is, of course, welcome, but training merely to win a match can lead to the deterioration of this dynamic and powerful art. The need to build true proficiency on a solid foundation, I feel, is more important than ever. I feel that karate should be viewed from a broad standpoint. From the point of its development as a modern martial art and from the physical education aspect also, the ultimate goal of karate should be the attainment of a developed moral character built through hard and diligent training.

Systematic and scientific training is also essential. Faulty training methods can result in acquiring bad habits or even in physical injury. However, the techniques which took years to perfect in the past can be mastered in half the time with a good training manual. Hard training is necessary to obtain proficiency, but thoughtless, unsystematic training will do more harm than good.

My experience in teaching students from Western countries after the war has also provided me with many valuable hints, such as the habit of seeking answers to questions from the fields of physiology and body kinetics. In this book I have tried to explain the execution of techniques based on these principles.

I realize that karate is difficult to master without a good instructor to teach the fine points. The photographs in this book provide step-by-step instructions to each technique and should be an adequate guide to help the student learn good karate. Common faults are also shown as a guide to what should not be done.

I take this opportunity to thank Tsuru Shobo Publishing Co. for the painstaking photography and for the publication of the Japanese language edition of this book, Mr. Mineo Higuchi and Mr. Herman Kauz for their efforts in translation, and finally Kodansha International for making this English edition possible.

I truly hope that the reader will follow the book carefully, train hard, and obtain proficiency in this great art.

August, 1966

MASATOSHI NAKAYAMA

Karate–Yesterday and Today

THE ORIGIN of karate dates back more than a thousand years. When Dharma was at the Shao Lin monastery in China, he taught his students physical training methods in order to build endurance and physical strength required to carry out the rigid discipline that was part of their religion. This physical training method was further developed and adapted to become what is known today as the Shao Lin art of fighting. This martial art was imported to Okinawa and blended with the indigenous fighting techniques of the islands. The lord of ancient Okinawa and later the feudal lord of Kagoshima, on the southernmost tip of Kyushu in Japan, banned the use of weapons, thus giving rise to the development of "empty-hand" fighting and self-defense techniques. This martial art, due to its Chinese origin, was called karate, written in characters with the literal meaning "Chinese hand." The modern master of this art, Funakoshi Gichin, who died in 1957 at the age of eighty-eight, changed the characters to mean literally "empty hand." Funakoshi, however, chose the character for its meaning in Zen Buddhist philosophy: "rendering oneself empty." To the master, karate was a martial art, but it was also a means of building character. He wrote: "As a mirror's polished surface reflects whatever stands before it and a quiet valley carries even small sounds, so must the student of karate render his mind empty of selfishness and wickedness in an effort to react appropriately toward anything he might encounter. This is the meaning of *kara*, or 'empty,' of karate."

Karate was first introduced to the Japanese public in 1922, when Funakoshi, who was then professor at the Okinawa Teacher's College, was invited to lecture and demonstrate at an exhibition of traditional martial arts sponsored by the Ministry of Education. His demonstration so impressed the audience that he was flooded with requests to teach in Tokyo. Instead of returning to Okinawa, Funakoshi taught karate at various universities and at the Kōdōkan, the mecca of Judo, until he was able to establish the Shōtōkan in 1936, a great landmark in the history of karate in Japan.

The Japan Karate Association was established in 1955 with Funakoshi as chief instructor. At that time, the organization had only a few members and a handful of instructors who had studied karate under the then aged master. The Association was approved as a corporation by the Ministry of Education in 1958. In that same year, the Association held the first all-Japan karate championship tournament, now an annual event, helping to establish karate as a competitive sport. Having experienced tremendous growth, the Association now boasts a membership of 100,000 active karate students and approximately 300 affiliated karate clubs throughout the world.

The role of karate in the modern age is multiple. As a practical means of self-defense, it is widely taught in private clubs, and in Japan it is a part of the training program for policemen and members of the armed forces. A great number of colleges now include karate in their physical education programs, and an increasing number of women are learning its techniques. In Japan and elsewhere in the world, moreover, karate is gaining great popularity as a competitive sport, one which stresses mental discipline as well as physical prowess. What was originally developed in the Orient as a martial art, then, has survived and changed through the centuries to become not only a highly effective means of unarmed self-defense, but also an exciting, challenging sport enjoyed by enthusiasts throughout the world.

Introduction

BASIC PRINCIPLES UNDERLYING KARATE TECHNIQUES

Tsuki (punching), *uchi* (striking), *keri* (kicking), and *uke* (blocking) are the fundamental karate techniques. They are at once the beginning and the final goal of karate. Students can easily learn to perform these basic movements in little more than two months, but perfection in their performance may be impossible. Therefore, students must practice regularly and employ maximum concentration and effort in the performance of each movement. However, practice will not achieve its object if it is undertaken incorrectly. Unless students learn techniques on a scientific basis, under an instructor employing a systematic and properly scheduled training system, their efforts will be in vain. Karate training can be considered scientific only when it is conducted on the basis of correct physical and physiological principles.

Surprisingly, an examination of the karate techniques which our predecessors created and refined through continuous study and practice reveals that these techniques accord with modern scientific principles. However, further refinement is always possible. We must try to analyze our techniques in an unceasing effort to improve.

The following points are of primary importance in the study of karate.

● *Form, Balance and Center of Gravity*

Karate is not the only sport that concentrates on the optimum utilization of the human body or embraces principles taught in physics and physiology. All the martial arts and most other sports depend on correct form for the effectiveness of their techniques. In baseball, good batting form is necessary to attain a high batting average. A fencer spends years perfecting movements which, to the layman, look easy. Such practice results in body movement, or form, which is physically and physiologically correct. Correct form is especially important in karate. All parts of the body must harmonize to provide the stability necessary to sustain the shock of delivering a kick or punch.

The karate student must often stand on one foot to attack or defend. Thus, balance is of prime importance. If the feet are placed far apart, with a consequent lowering of the center of gravity, a kick or punch will be stronger. However, it is easier to move if the center of gravity is somewhat higher and the feet closer together rather than spread to the maximum possible extent. Therefore, although stability is important, there is a point beyond which it is not worth going. If the student is overly concerned with stability, he will lose elasticity. If he bends his knees too much to maintain balance, his kick will not be effective. Thus, the position of the body and, consequently, the center of gravity, depends upon the circumstances.

The center of gravity is always shifting. Sometimes body weight is evenly distributed between both feet, and sometimes there is more on one foot than on the other. When performing *yoko-geri* (side kick), the weight is completely shifted to one foot. In this case, the student must stand firmly on one leg, otherwise the shock of delivering the kick will upset his balance.

However, if he stands on one foot for too long, his opponent can easily attack. Therefore, his balance must be shifted constantly from one foot to the other. His center of gravity must shift quickly from right to left and back again to avoid giving the opponent an opportunity to attack. At the same time, the student must constantly look for an opening in his opponent's defense.

● *Power and Speed*

The possession of muscular strength alone will not enable one to excel in the martial arts or, for that matter, in any sport. The effective use of strength is important. The application of power to any movement depends on a number of factors. One of the most important of these is speed.

The basic punching and kicking techniques of karate achieve their power by the concentration of maximum force at the moment of impact. This concentration of force depends greatly upon the speed with which techniques are executed. Other things being equal, greater speed will result in increased power. The punch of an advanced karateist can travel at a speed of 43 feet per second, and generate power to destroy equal to 1,500 pounds.

Speed is an important element in the application of power, but speed cannot achieve its greatest effect without good control.

The kind of movement needed in fundamental karate techniques is not one which will move a heavy object slowly, but one which will move a light object with maximum speed. Thus, the strong but slow exercise of power necessary to lift a barbell is not as effective in karate as the power developed by hitting the punching board (*makiwara*) with great speed.

Another principle to remember is that greater speed can be generated if power travels a longer route to its target. For example, in kicking, the knee of the kicking leg should be bent as much as possible and the body so placed in relation to the target that the leg will be fully stretched at the moment of impact. The longer the course the leg travels to the target, the stronger the kick will be.

In order to increase power and speed, it is necessary to practice responding to sudden and unrehearsed attacks. Such practice, together with an understanding and application of the dynamics of movement, will help shorten reaction time.

● *Concentration of Power*

A punch or kick will be weak if applied with the arm or leg alone. To achieve maximum power it is necessary to use the strength of all parts of the body simultaneously. When punching or kicking, power moves from the center of the body, the major muscles, to the extremities, ending in the hand or foot. This power moves from one part of the body to the next at a speed of 1/100 of a second. The whole movement from beginning to end takes only .15 to .18 of a second if the momentum possible in this action is correctly exploited. Training should be conducted so that all available strength is focused in the foot when kicking or in the hand when punching.

It is important that the various muscles and tendons are kept loose and relaxed to permit instant response to changing circumstances. If the muscles are already tense, they cannot be further tensed at the moment of focus.

Power concentrated at the time of focus must be instantly released to prepare for the succeeding action. Constant training in alternately tensing and relaxing the body is very important to acquire proficiency in the application of karate techniques. (See "Analysis of Karate Movements" at the end of this book.)

● *Role of Muscular Power*
Power to move the body is supplied by the muscles. Well-trained, powerful, and elastic muscles are mandatory in karate. Even if the student is well-versed in karate theory and knows the principles of the dynamics of movement, his technique will be weak if his muscles are not strong enough. Therefore, constant training is necessary to strengthen the muscles of the body.

If karate training is to be conducted scientifically, it is also necessary to know which muscles are employed in the execution of a particular technique. When practicing a new technique, students sometimes use unnecessary muscles or muscles which actually hinder the performance of the technique. Therefore, beginners must carefully follow the advice of their teachers. When the proper muscles operate fully and harmoniously, the technique will be strong and effective. On the other hand, if unnecessary muscles operate there will result, at the very least, a loss of energy, and at worst an ineffective technique.

Finally, the speed of muscular contraction is important, because the faster a muscle is tensed the greater will be the power produced.

● *Rhythm*
An essential element in the performance of techniques in the martial arts and other sports is rhythm. The proper execution of a series of movements in any sport is impossible without rhythm. Also, the rhythm evident in the movements of athletes is more complicated than, and cannot be expressed in terms of, musical rhythm. It is essential for the karate student to learn correct rhythm in both the basic techniques and in the more advanced sparring (*kumite*).

Rhythm is especially necessary in the performance of formal exercise (*kata*). We have been taught since early times that the three most important elements in *kata* performance are the application of strength at the correct time, the control of speed in techniques and from technique to technique, and the smooth transition of the body from one technique to the next. These requirements cannot be fulfilled without rhythm. The *kata* performance of a person advanced in karate is powerful, rhythmical, and consequently, beautiful.

● *Timing*
Correct timing is of utmost importance in applying techniques. If timing is faulty, the technique will fail. A kick or punch which is directed at the target either too early or too late is often fruitless.

The start of a technique is of first importance in any consideration of timing. To start their particular movements more effectively, baseball players and golfers condition their swings with practice swings. However, there is no opportunity for anything like a practice swing in karate, where the outcome can be decided in an instant. A failure in timing could be disastrous.

The attack in karate must be launched with the hands and feet in the usual position of readiness or defense. Obviously, the hands and feet must always be positioned so that techniques can be easily and quickly applied. Immediately after the application of a technique, they must be returned to their former position, ready for the following movement. Moreover, during the course of these movements the body must be kept relaxed, but alert, with the muscles full of energy and ready for any eventuality.

● *Lower Abdomen and Hips*
Coaches of modern sports constantly stress the role of the hips in furnishing maximum power to any movement. For example, they say, "Hit with your hips," or "Throw with your hips," or "Get your hips into it."

In Japan the importance of the *tanden* has been taught from early times. Teachers of the martial arts, and those of other arts and disciplines, have constantly emphasized the importance of the *tanden* in achieving competence. This region was emphasized because it was felt that here was centered the human spirit, and that this area provided the basis of power and balance.

The *tanden* actually is that area behind the navel, in the center of the body. When standing erect, the body's center of gravity is located here. If the stance is correct in karate, the center of gravity will be found in the *tanden*. A correct stance will enable the student to maintain the balance of both the upper and lower parts of his body, resulting in harmonious interplay of the muscles and a minimum loss of energy.

If the power concentrated in the *tanden* is brought into play in executing karate techniques, the pelvic and hip bones will be firmly supported by the thighs, and the trunk by the spine. This interlocking support will produce strong techniques.

The center of the body, i.e., the lower abdominal area and the hips, plays a great part in our various movements. Therefore, try to punch with the hips, kick with the hips, and block with the hips.

Part I
The Fundamental
Techniques

Instructor H. Ochi, fourth dan, demonstrates a yoko-geri in masterful form on a cliff at Shimoda.

M. Ueki, instructor Fuchu Air Force Base (right), scores with a right tsuki an instant before K. Kisaka, fourth dan counters with a right age-zuki.

M. Ueki, fourth dan, counters with a mae-geri to score against K. Kisaka in the 8th All-Japan Karate Championships in Tokyo, 1965.

Chapter 1

Stance and Posture

IMPORTANCE OF CORRECT FORM

If the body lacks balance and stability, offensive and defensive techniques will be ineffective. The ability to defend against an attack under any circumstances depends largely upon the maintenance of correct form.

Stance in karate is mainly concerned with the position of the lower part of the body. Powerful, fast, accurate, and smoothly executed techniques can be performed only from a strong and stable base. The upper body must be firmly settled on this strong base, and the back kept straight, or perpendicular to the ground. Although an effective attack is impossible without a strong stance, it is only necessary to assume this position just before delivering an attack. If the student concentrates too much on remaining in a firm and stable position, he will lose mobility.

REQUIREMENTS OF A GOOD STANCE

In addition to the above, the following points are closely related to the development of a good stance. The student must:

A. Be well balanced when applying offensive or defensive techniques;
B. Rotate his hips smoothly when executing techniques;
C. Apply his techniques with the greatest possible speed; and
D. Insure that the muscles used in attack or defense work together harmoniously.

Therefore, the first consideration is the establishment of a strong and stable base. From this base all parts of the body must work together harmoniously as a single unit. In other words, the feet, legs, trunk, arms, and hands must be well controlled individually, but at the same time work together as a unit.

It is important also that the muscles necessary to perform a particular technique respond fully, and that those not used be kept relaxed. If your stance is incorrect, the harmonious interaction of your muscles will be absent and your techniques less effective. Poor form brings unnecessary muscles into play, muscles which often hamper speedy and powerful movements. Strong, fast techniques depend for their execution upon a firm base. Further, the delicate control necessary in karate is only possible with a stable and correct stance.

Most karate students have only an incomplete knowledge of stance. Many are unfamiliar with the varieties possible. Even in the case of a particular stance, there is a real difference in its form at various times. For example, the form of a particular stance is different in the ready position from its form at the time a technique is applied. The form of the stance immediately after the technique has been applied again differs from the preceding two. There is a delicate change at each stage, although the form looks almost the same.

The concept of one definite stance for a particular occasion is foreign to karate. The stance chosen varies according to the circumstances. However, it must be natural and it must allow one to move freely in all directions and to assume any position.

A few concrete examples can help illustrate the above points. In *zenkutsu-dachi* (front stance), there is an important difference between the stance as a preparation for applying a technique and the same stance at the moment of application. In the former instance the knee of the front leg must be bent and the muscles in the thighs and calves of both legs relaxed to permit flexible and quick movement. However, the instant a technique is applied, the muscles of the legs must tense to strengthen the hold of the feet on the ground and to give power to the movement.

Furthermore, in either the front stance or *neko-ashi-dachi* (cat stance), the position taken must not be so low that the muscles become tense, inflexible, or stiff. If this occurs it will be impossible to move quickly when necessary.

It is detrimental to the development of beginners if, instead of concentrating on basic training, they attempt to imitate the stance used by advanced students. The advanced may stand very lightly with their hips in a relatively high position. However, they can change this stance in an instant to a very strong and firm one with the hips low. It is difficult for beginners to duplicate this change, for the obvious reason that advanced students have spent a much longer time practicing. If beginners stand like the advanced, they will lose their balance at the moment of focusing the technique. Remember that in addition to stability while in a ready, or defensive, position, the stance must provide enough strength and firmness to withstand the shock caused by the application of techniques.

Stance changes according to the direction of movement and the kind of technique applied. The exhaustive studies of our predecessors have resulted in a number of stances which form the basis of present-day karate.

The following are the main stances in karate:

Shizen-tai (natural position) includes *musubi-dachi* (informal attention stance, feet turned out), *heisoku-dachi* (informal attention stance), *hachiji-dachi* (open-leg stance), *teiji-dachi* (T stance), and *heikō-dachi* (parallel stance).

Zenkutsu-dachi (front stance)

Kōkutsu-dachi (back stance)

Kiba-dachi (straddle-leg stance)

Shiko-dachi (square stance)

Fudō-dachi (rooted stance)

Neko-ashi-dachi (cat stance)

Sanchin-dachi (hour-glass stance)

Hangetsu-dachi (half-moon stance)

Each stance was designed for a particular purpose. Therefore, progress in learning will be slow if beginners do not adhere strictly to the form of each stance. Do not permit the form of a particular stance to deteriorate so that it is difficult to tell it from another. Pay strict attention to the requirements of each stance.

Certain training methods are useful in learning a stance. For example, it is helpful to keep the same stance under tension for a long time. Another method is to alternately tense and relax the muscles for short intervals while holding a stance. This latter method also helps to develop the coordination and to cultivate the feeling necessary for correctly focusing a technique.

When learning a stance it is helpful to practice the offensive and defensive techniques which are best delivered from it.

**Heisoku-dachi
(informal attention
stance)**

**Musubi-dachi
(informal attention
stance, feet turned
out)**

**Hachiji-dachi
(open-leg stance)**

**Uchi-hachiji-dachi
(inverted open-leg
stance)**

**Heikō-dachi
(parallel stance)**

**Teiji-dachi
(T stance)**

Renoji-dachi
(L stance)

Zenkutsu-dachi
(front stance)

Kōkutsu-dachi
(back stance)

Kiba-dachi
(straddle-leg stance)

Shiko-dachi
(square stance)

Fudō-dachi (rooted stance)

**Neko-ashi-dachi
(cat stance)**   **Sanchin-dachi
(hour-glass stance)**   **Hangetsu-dachi (half-moon stance)**

Shizen-tai (natural position)

In *shizen-tai* the body remains relaxed but alert, in the sense that potential for movement is present. There is no special design or intention, but from the natural position any position of attack or defense can quickly be assumed. Therefore, the knees must be relaxed and flexible, and the weight evenly distributed between both legs. The position of the body and the feet changes in the various forms of *shizen-tai*, but the principle of alert relaxation remains. The following are possible stances in *shizen-tai:*

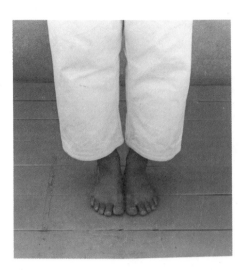

Stances in shizen-tai

**Heisoku-dachi
(informal attention
stance)**

Heisoku-dachi (informal attention stance)—Keep the feet parallel and touching one another. Knees are straight, but relaxed.

Musubi-dachi (informal attention stance, feet turned out)—This stance is similar in every respect to *heisoku-dachi*, except that the feet are pointed outward at 45 degree angles with the heels together.

**Musubi-dachi
(informal attention stance,
feet turned out)**

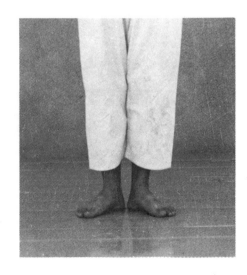

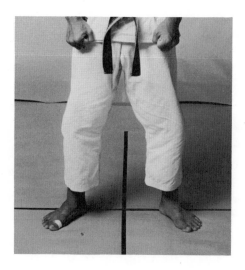

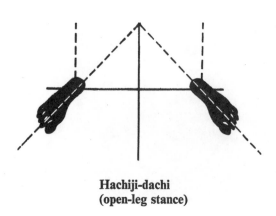

**Hachiji-dachi
(open-leg stance)**

Hachiji-dachi (open-leg stance)—This stance is perhaps the most natural and comfortable of all the stances. Place the feet so that the heels are separated by a distance roughly equal to the width of the hips, and point the toes outward at 45 degree angles. One foot should not be ahead of the other. A straight line should bisect both heels.

Heikō-dachi (parallel stance)—This stance is similar to the open-leg stance, but the feet are kept parallel to one another.

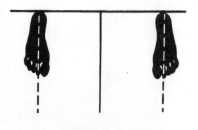

**Heikō-dachi
(parallel stance)**

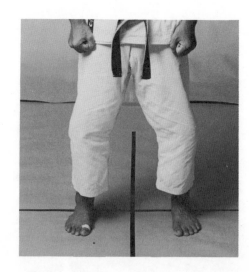

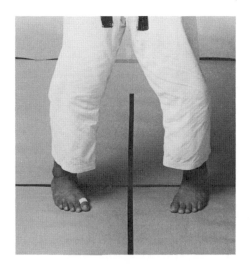

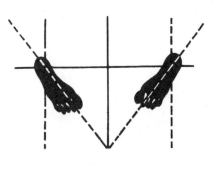

**Uchi-hachiji-dachi
(inverted open-leg
stance)**

Uchi-hachiji-dachi (inverted open-leg stance)—In this stance the heels are separated, as in the open-leg stance and the parallel stance, by the width of the hips, but the feet are turned inward at 45 degree angles.

Teiji-dachi (T stance)—The feet here roughly form a T, with back foot, the top of the T, turned slightly inward. A distance of about 12 inches should separate the heel of the front foot from the instep of the rear foot. When the right foot is forward, this position is called *migi-teiji-dachi* (right T stance) and also *migi-shizen-tai* (right natural position). When the left foot is forward, it is called *hidari-teiji-dachi* (left T stance) and also *hidari-shizen-tai* (left natural position).

**Teiji-dachi
(T stance)**

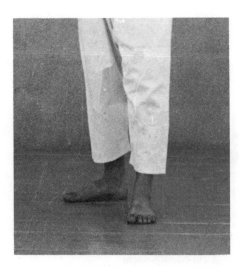

**Renoji-dachi
(L stance)**

Renoji-dachi (L stance)—The feet form an "L" so that a line roughly bisecting the front will pass alongside the back of the heel of the rear foot.

Zenkutsu-dachi (front stance)

● *General Considerations*

Be sure there is a big enough space between the front and rear foot. Lower the hips. Bend the front knee so it is over the front foot as in the diagram. Keep the back leg straight. Maintain a straight back with the upper body perpendicular to the ground. It is possible to face either directly forward or at *hanmi* (half-front-facing position). In the latter position maintain the hips and shoulders at a 45 degree angle to the front, but face directly forward.

The front stance is a strong stance to the front and is especially effective when power must be directed forward. It is used to block an attack coming from the front, but it is also a strong position from which to attack a target directly ahead.

Zenkutsu-dachi (front stance)

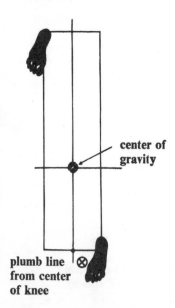

center of
gravity

plumb line
from center
of knee

32

**Front knee faces
outside and front
foot not firm**

**Front knee bent
too far and heel
of rear foot raised**

● *Specific Points to Remember*

1. Keep a distance of about 32 inches between the front and back feet. Maintain a width between the feet equivalent to the width of the hips.

2. Tighten the ankles and knees of both legs and keep the soles of the feet firmly in contact with the ground.

3. Point the front foot slightly inward. Turn the back foot to the front as much as possible so that both feet point in about the same direction.

4. Place the knee of the front leg in such a position that a plumb line dropped from its center will fall just to the inside of the ball of the foot.

5. Distribute the body weight so that the front leg supports about 60 and the rear leg 40 percent. The center of gravity is thus closer to the front foot.

● *Common Faults*

1. Too much weight is placed on the front foot, and the heel of the rear foot is not firmly on the ground. This undermines stability.

2. One foot is placed directly behind the other, reducing the distance between the feet to less than the width of the hips. This lessens stability and balance to the side. Moreover, balance to the front and to the rear will be weakened if the feet are placed wider apart than the distance between the hips.

3. The front foot points outward instead of slightly inward or the rear foot points to the side instead of forward. These faults impair stability.

4. The front knee is straightened instead of being bent. This raises the level of the hips and reduces stability.

5. The knee of the leading leg moves too much to one side or the other of the point marked in the diagram. This weakens the knee in the direction of the error.

6. The front ankle is not fully flexed. This causes a corresponding looseness in the knee and results in an unstable position.

Kōkutsu-dachi (back stance)

  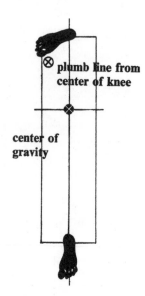

⊗ plumb line from
center of knee

center of
gravity

● *General Considerations*

Keep the hips low, bend the knee of the rear leg properly, and extend the forward leg to the front. This stance is strong to the rear and very useful in blocking. It is an ideal position from which to block an attack coning from the front and then, by changing to the front stance, to deliver an immediate counterattack.

● *Specific Points to Remember*

1. Separate the front and rear foot by a distance of about 32 inches, and place the rear foot in a position such that its heel would be intersected by a line drawn through the center of the front foot.

2. Flex the ankle of the rear leg and keep the bottom of the foot firmly on the ground. Place the heel of the front foot on the ground, but not firmly so.

3. Point the front foot directly forward. Turn the rear foot to the side, but force it slightly forward or inward. Be sure the ankles form a 90 degree angle in relation to one another.

4. Force the knee of the rear leg outward as much as possible so that a plumb line dropped from the knee will hit the spot marked in the diagram. Maintain an outward tension in this knee to give strength to the stance.

5. Locate the center of gravity so that the rear leg bears 70 and the front 30 percent of the body weight.

● *Common Faults*

1. The front knee is bent too much. This puts the weight on the front leg.

2. The feet are too close together. This forces the hips to rise.

3. The front foot points in other than a forward direction, or the back foot points to the rear.

4. The ankle and the knee of the rear leg are relaxed. This causes the body to sink down on this leg.

5. The body weight moves too much onto the back leg so that the position of the knee shifts from that recommended in the diagram.

Kiba-dachi (straddle-leg stance)

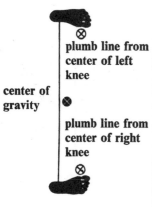

center of gravity

plumb line from center of left knee

plumb line from center of right knee

● *General Considerations*

To perform *kiba-dachi* properly, bend the knees, keep the upper body perpendicular to the ground, and face straight ahead. This position roughly resembles that taken by a man astride a horse. The straddle-leg stance is strong to the side and used when applying techniques to the side. For example, *empi-uchi* (elbow strike) and *uraken-uchi* (back-fist strike) are delivered from this position.

● *Specific Points to Remember*

1. Maintain the upper body in a position perpendicular to the ground, and do not lean either to the front or to the rear, otherwise stability will be impaired.

2. Force the feet inward to overcome the tendency for them to turn outward.

3. Be sure that the position of the knees corresponds to that marked in the diagram, and that the soles of the feet are placed firmly on the ground.

4. Flex the ankles and knees so that the knees remain in the correct position.

5. Keep the hips low. If the knees are straightened, the hips will rise.

6. Keep the buttocks flexed, but prevent their extension to the rear. If this occurs the upper part of the body will lean forward.

● *Common Faults*

1. The distance between the feet is appreciably greater or smaller than 32 inches. However, remember that this width varies according to body structure.

2. Not all of the sole of the foot is in firm contact with the ground.

3. The feet point outward. Keep the feet pointing forward and slightly inwards.

4. The knees point inward. Direct the knees forward and outward so that a plumb line dropped from the center of the knee falls just inside of the big toe.

5. The center of gravity shifting from the point marked in the diagram.

6. One leg bears more weight than the other. Support the body weight equally between both legs.

7. The knees are permitted to relax. Flex the knees and direct power outward to the side. Simultaneously, flex the buttocks.

Sanchin-dachi (hour-glass stance)

  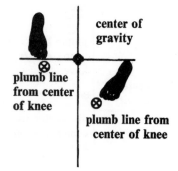

center of gravity

plumb line from center of knee

plumb line from center of knee

● *General Considerations*
The right foot is lightly behind the left so that an imaginary horizontal line would touch the back of the heel of the left foot and the front of the big toe of the right. Both knees must be bent and turned inward. As in the foregoing stances, keep the upper body perpendicular to the ground and tense the lower abdomen. Despite the relatively narrow position of the feet, this stance provides a strong base for defensive techniques. From this stance one can easily move into any other stance and go in any direction. The knees in this position are flexed inward, in contrast to the back stance and the straddle-leg stance where the force is directed outward.

● *Specific Points to Remember*
1.   Separate the feet by a distance equal to the width of the hips. Keep the heel of the front foot on the same line as the big toe of the rear. (See diagram.)
2.   Point the front foot inward at an angle of 45 degrees. Point the rear foot directly forward.
3.   Bend the knees so that a plumb line dropped from the center of each knee falls at the points indicated in the diagram.
4.   Tense the ankles and press the knees inward. Be especially careful to tighten the knees, because the feet are relatively narrowly spaced.
5.   Tense the muscles of the inner part of the thighs and tense the buttocks.
6.   Be sure the center of gravity falls at a point midway between the feet. Body weight, therefore, should be distributed equally between both legs.

● *Common Faults*
1.   Do not bend the knees inward too much. Doing so will weaken the outside of the knees and reduce stability.
2.   Do not lean forward, allowing the heels to leave the ground.
3.   Do not straighten the knees, otherwise the hips will be too high.
4.   Do not allow the knees to relax.

Shiko-dachi (square stance)

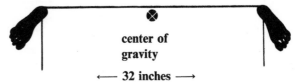

center of
gravity

⟵ 32 inches ⟶

Shiko-dachi (square stance)
This stance is just like the straddle-leg stance except that the feet are turned outward at an angle of 45 degrees and the hips are lower. A plumb line dropped from
the center of the knees would hit a point midway between the feet.

Hangetsu-dachi (half-moon stance)

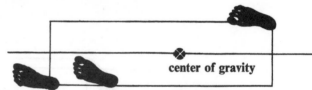

For front stance advance foot to this point

Hangetsu-dachi (half-moon stance)

Hangetsu-dachi is a stance midway between the front stance and the hour-glass stance. The placing of the feet is almost the same as in the front stance but the distance between the feet in *hangetsu* is shorter. The method of forcing the knees inward, however, is similar to the hour-glass stance. This stance is useful for both attack and defense, but tends to be favored for defense.

The *hangetsu kata* (half-moon formal exercise) conveys a rhythmical feeling. The participants stand in *hangetsu-dachi* (see photo above).

Fudō-dachi (rooted stance)

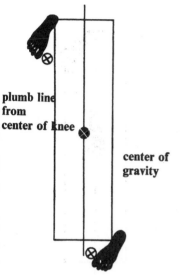   

plumb line
from
center of knee

center of
gravity

plumb line from
center of knee

Fudō-dachi (rooted stance)

This stance is also known as *sochin-dachi*. It is a combination of the front stance and the straddle-leg stance. The illustrations show a great similarity to the straddle-leg stance except for a difference in the direction in which the feet point. The rooted stance is a firm and strong stance, giving the impression of a deeply rooted tree. Merely by changing the direction in which the feet point, this stance can be turned into the straddle-leg stance. To assume this stance, both knees must be bent to the same degree. The rooted stance is effective for blocking a strong attack and delivering an immediate counterattack.

In this stance exert force outward at the knees, and distribute the body weight equally between both legs.

Neko-ashi-dachi (cat stance)

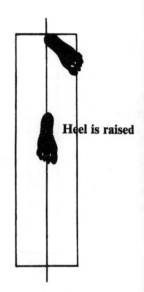

Heel is raised

Neko-ashi-dachi (cat stance)

To assume *neko-ashi-dachi*, begin from back stance and withdraw the front foot until the heel is raised and the ball of the foot lightly touches the floor. Turn the knee of the leading foot slightly inward so the thigh protects the groin. Point the rear foot forward at a 45 degree angle and bend the knee. Support most of the body weight with the rear leg.

This form adapts itself well to flexible and light-footed body movements. For example, use the cat stance to move out of range of the opponent's attack and then counterattack with the front foot. It is a very elastic stance. This stance should give the impression of the crouch of a cat ready to spring. It is often seen in free type sparring (*jiyū kumite*).

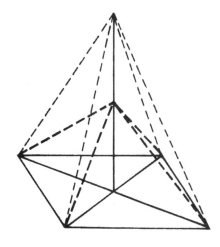

Stability depends upon stance base area and center of gravity

The stability of a stance depends to a great degree on the area included within its base. For example, the back stance is more stable than the cat stance, and the front stance provides more stability than the back stance. This is because the base area of the back stance is greater than that of the cat stance, and the front stance base is larger than that of the back stance.

However, we must also consider the position of the center of gravity. As the center of gravity is lowered, stability increases. Therefore, stance in which the hips are relatively low tends to be more stable than those in which the hips are high. For instance, the rooted stance, the front stance, the straddle-leg stance, and the square stance all provide great stability not only because the area of their bases are large, but also because the center of gravity is low in these positions. Further, a particular stance gains or loses stability as the center of gravity is raised or lowered. Thus, the front stance is more stable if the hips are low than if they are high.

Another point is that the body will be more stable supported by both legs than if it is supported only by one. For example, the hour-glass stance is stronger than the front stance or the cat stance because the first uses two legs as a base, while the latter two depend mainly on one leg.

The proper stance to employ depends upon the situation. There is no one stance which is suitable for all occasions.

STANCE DEVELOPMENT

After digesting the foregoing general points, begin actual training in developing correct stance. The best method is to assume one stance and then to move into related stances by pivoting without lifting the feet. Be sure the hips do not move up or down as one stance changes to another. Keep your hands on your hips during these movements. Refer to the diagram on page 43 and do the following:

A. Assume a straddle-leg stance facing A.

B. Keep the left knee bent and straighten the right knee, shifting the weight slightly toward the left and changing the direction of the feet toward the left. You should now be facing B and should have assumed a front stance.

C. Return to the straddle-leg stance by bending the right knee and facing A. The center of gravity returns to that point in the diagram relating to the straddle-leg stance.

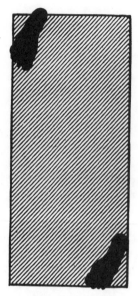

**Zenkutsu-dachi
(front stance)**

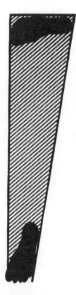

**Kōkutsu-dachi
(back stance)**

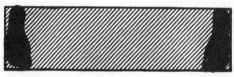

**Kiba-dachi
(straddle-leg
stance)**

**Neko-ashi-dachi
(cat stance)**

**Sanchin-dachi
(hour-glass stance)**

D. Keep the right knee bent and slightly straighten the left knee. Turn the left foot outward toward C and shift your weight onto your right leg. You should now be facing C and have assumed the back stance.

E. Return to the straddle-leg stance by turning the left foot, bending the left knee, shifting your weight evenly onto both legs, and facing A.

F. Practice the foregoing movements, turning to the right instead of the left.

After the above practice has become fairly smooth, stand in the natural position and then move into various stances. For example, from the natural stance assume a front stance and then return to the natural stance. When moving into the front stance the front foot describes a kind of half circle beginning from its initial position to a point close to the other foot and then forward to its terminal position. Withdraw the foot along the same route. Be sure the foot is not raised and remains lightly in contact with the ground throughout the movement so that an attack can be delivered at any point during the movement.

All parts of the body must begin and end their actions at the same time. For example, to step forward with the leg while the upper body remains behind results in a moment of weakness which lasts until the upper body moves forward. The body must move as a unit.

Practice in assuming various stances from the natural stance helps to train the body to move quickly and smoothly but still maintain stability and balance.

Training for Zenkutsu-dachi (front stance)

1. Assume the open-leg stance of the natural position with the hands on the hips.

2. Slide your right foot forward and assume the right-front stance. Make sure that in sliding forward, your foot remains lightly in contact with the ground. Imagine that the thickness of a sheet of paper separates the sole of your foot from the ground.

3. Return the right foot to its original position and once again assume the natural position.

4. Slide the left foot forward and assume the left-front stance.

5. Return to the original position by moving the foot back again.

6. Slide the right foot one step to the rear and assume the left-front position.

7. Return to the original position.

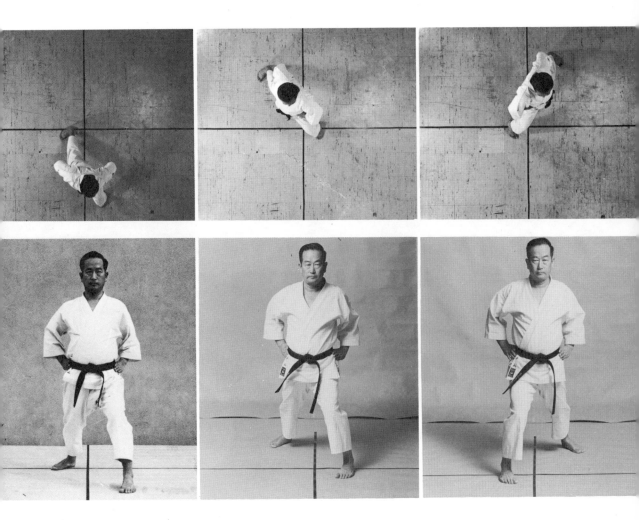

8.   Slide the left foot one step to the rear and assume the right-front position.

9.   Return to the natural position.

10.   Slide the left foot to your left, turn your body to the left and assume the left-front stance.

11.   Return to the natural position.

12.   Slide the right foot to your right, turn your body to the right and assume the right-front position.

13.   Return to the natural position.

After practicing these movements, try moving diagonally forward and to the rear. Practice first on one side by moving the left foot, and then on the other by moving the right. Training for the rooted stance can be accomplished in the same manner.

Training for Kōkutsu-dachi (back stance)

1. Assume the natural position with the hands on the hips.
2. Slide the right foot diagonally to the rear. Assume the right-back stance.
3. Return to the natural position.
4. Slide the left foot diagonally to the rear. Assume left-back stance.
5. Return to the natural position.
6. Slide the right foot to the rear and assume the right-back stance.
7. Return to the natural position.
8. Slide the left foot to the rear and assume the left-back stance.
9. Return to the natural position.
10. Slide the right foot to the right side, turn the body to the left and assume the right-back stance.
11. Return to the natural position.
12. Slide the left foot to the left side, turn the body to the right, and assume the left-back stance.
13. Return to the natural position.

Training for Neko-ashi-dachi (cat stance)

**Front foot bears too
much weight**

**Front foot too far for-
ward, and back knee too
far back**

Practice moving into the cat stance in all directions as was done in the case of the back stance. However, when moving your right foot back in the cat stance, also withdraw your left foot one half-step and raise the heel.

To return to the natural position, first return the left foot to its original position and then move the right foot. This principle applies to the opposite side of the body as well.

Training Method for Kiba-dachi (straddle-leg stance)

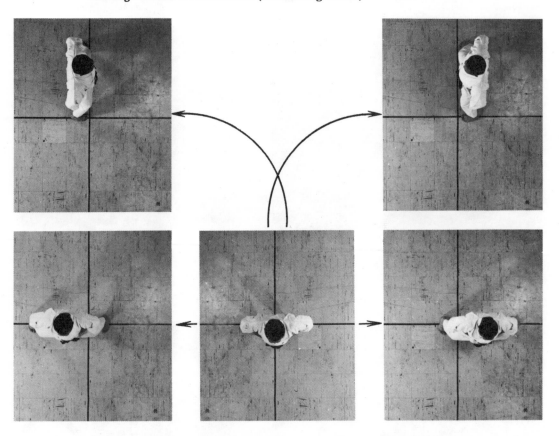

1. Assume the open-leg stance of the natural position with the hands on the hips.
2. Leaving your left foot in place, shift the hips to the right and slide your right foot to the right. Face forward and assume the straddle-leg stance.
3. Return to the natural position.
4. Leaving your right foot in place, shift the hips to the left and slide your left foot to the left. Face forward and assume the straddle-leg stance.
2. Return to the natural position.
4. Leaving your right foot in place, shift the hips to the left and slide your left foot to the left. Face forward and assume the straddle-leg stance.
5. Return to the natural position.
6. Slide the right foot to the rear, pivot on your left foot and turn the body 90 degrees to the right by shifting the hips. Assume the straddle-leg stance facing 90 degrees to the right in relation to the original position.
7. Return to the natural position.
8. Slide the left foot to the rear, pivot on your right foot and turn the body 90 degrees to the left by shifting the hips. Assume the straddle-leg stance facing 90 degrees to the left in relation to the original position.
9. Return to the natural position.

Training in Various Stances

1. Assume the natural position, with the hands on the hips.
2. Slide the left foot forward and assume the left-front stance.
3. Return to the natural position.
4. Slide the right foot forward and assume the right-front stance.

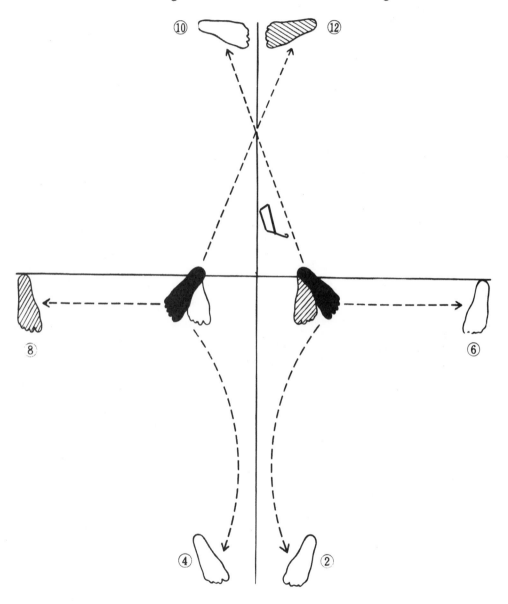

5. Return to the natural position.
6. Slide the left foot to the side and assume the straddle-leg stance.
7. Return to the natural position.
8. Slide the right foot to the side and assume the straddle-leg stance.
9. Return to the natural position.
10. Slide the left foot to the rear and assume the left-back stance.
11. Return to the natural position.
12. Slide the right foot to the rear and assume the right-back stance.
13. Return to the natural position.

Cat Stance to Front Stance

Rooted Stance to Front Stance

Back Stance to Front Stance

Transition from Stance to Stance

Each stance has its own special characteristics. A stance is most effective if it is used in that situation for which it was specifically designed. For example, if your opponent aims a punch at your head and you block his punch with *age-uke* (upper block), you should not assume the cat stance or the hour-glass stance. These stances tend to contract the body, placing it too far from the opponent to launch an instantaneous and powerful counterattack. However, the front stance ideally fulfills the necessary conditions. You are close enough to the opponent when blocking from this stance to launch an immediate and strong response.

Sometimes it is possible to block an attack using the back stance or the rooted stance and then to deliver an immediate counterattack simply by shifting the hips and assuming the front stance.

As your training progresses, you must become familiar with the characteristics of each stance and know the conditions for which a particular stance is best suited.

Rooted Stance to Front Stance

Back Stance to Front Stance

51

Front Stance—advancing and retreating

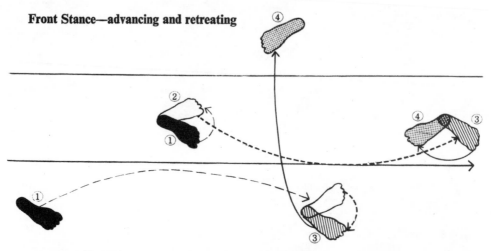

Stance Training in Continuous Movement
In general, when moving keep the hips at the same level and slide the feet lightly across the floor. To practice moving, first take five steps forward and then turn and take five steps in the opposite direction. Of course, it is also possible to retreat instead of turning, affording practice in moving away from an attack.

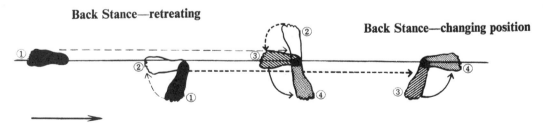

Back Stance—retreating

Back Stance—changing position

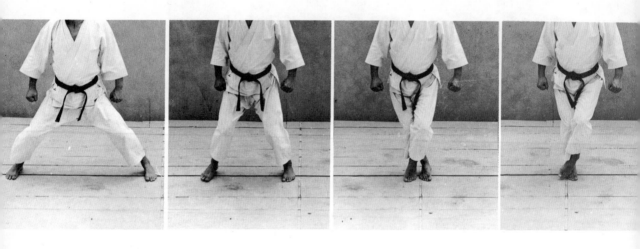

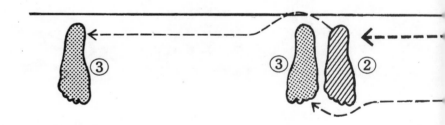

Straddle-leg Stance—moving to the side

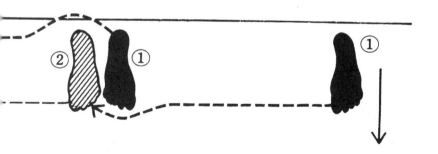

Hour-glass Stance—advancing

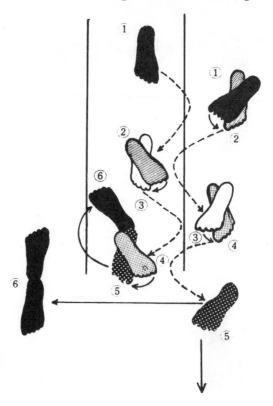

Chapter 2
Applying the Power in the Hips

The destructive force of karate is generated by turning the body, and especially by rotating the hips. In delivering a karate punch, just as in hitting a baseball or a golf ball, the smooth, swift, and level turn of the hips is essential to the effective application of power. You cannot throw an effective punch with arm and shoulder strength alone.

Rotating the Hips

Power generated by rotating the hips is conveyed to the backbone, then to the muscles of the chest and shoulders, and finally to the arm and fist, resulting in a powerful technique. The speed of the punch gains additional acceleration if the fist is driven forward with the intention of straightening the elbow. If these points are followed the fist should strike the target with maximum power.

A given amount of hip rotation results in a much larger motion at the extremities of the body, just as the turning of the drive shaft of a wheel creates a larger and faster movement at its outer surface. In a karate punch the trunk works as the drive shaft.

The abdominal muscles at the side play the major role in turning the hips. However, the power of the thigh muscles also contributes to smooth and powerful hip movements. In the photos on page 59, the left hip is withdrawn by the action of the abdominal muscles at the left side and the inner thigh muscles of the left leg. The muscles of the right side and the right thigh move the right hip forward. Be sure to keep the muscles of the sides relaxed and ready to rotate the hips instantly.

To increase the power and speed of a punch, turn the hips faster. Constant training will produce a sharp, snappy hip rotation. Remember that the hips can never be turned too fast.

The turn of the hips produces the driving power necessary for strong techniques. Therefore, a great deal of practice must go into producing good hip movements, even at the expense of practice in arm movements.

It is not easy to master correct hip rotation. Constant practice in the correct method is essential.

Persevere in spite of the monotony of practice. Learn the theory, because this is the starting point of karate.

Hips must turn on same level

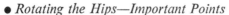

● *Rotating the Hips—Important Points*

1. Rotate the hips in one continuous movement, ensuring that throughout the turn they remain on the same level. One hip should not drop below the other.

2. Turn the shoulders at the same time as the hips. Do not turn the shoulders first and then follow with the hips.

3. When rotating the hips do not lean forward, thereby extending the buttocks to the rear. Keep the trunk perpendicular to the ground.

4. As illustrated, rotate the hips along the same horizontal plane during the turn.

5. To turn the hips fully, at the end of the movement twist the rear thigh around until its leading surface points directly forward.

● *Rotating the Hips—Training Method*

1.   Assume the front stance, with the hands on the hips. Face forward. Extend the elbows outward at the sides and point the thumbs in the direction of the backbone. Relax the shoulders, ensuring that they are not raised. Think of the lower abdomen as the center of power. Throw the chest out. Press the hipbones forward and upward with the thumbs.

2.   Assume *hanmi* (half-front-facing position). Without changing the position of the feet, the knees, or the level of the hips, turn the hips 45 degrees to the side. Perform the movement slowly to insure that the hips travel the correct path. The upper body must rotate with the movement of the hips.

3.   Face forward. Turn the body so it is again facing forward, rotating the hips with a smooth and level movement. At the instant the movement terminates, tense the previously relaxed muscles of the abdomen and chest. Simultaneously, fully flex the muscles of the rear leg.

4.   Assume *hanmi*. Relax the muscles and turn to the front-facing position, moving the hips smoothly and levelly. In the manner outlined above, move from the front facing position to *hanmi* and back again, repeating this action many times. As you become accustomed to this practice, gradually increase speed and power.

One hip drops below the other

It is also necessary to practice this movement in response to a command and to maintain proper rhythm.

● *Points to Avoid*

1.   When facing forward the upper body leans forward. Press the hipbones upward with the thumbs.

2.   In the *hanmi* position the leading hip is retracted and the upper body leans forward. Press the hipbone upward with the thumb of the hand on the trailing hip.

3.   After the turn from *hanmi* to the front facing position the shoulder extends beyond the hip. Tighten the muscles of the lower abdomen so that the body acts as a unit. Imagine that the upper body is like a single block of wood.

4.   When facing forward the knee of the rear leg bends and the heel of the foot rises. The hip has not been turned to the maximum extent. Tense the muscles of the leg to turn the hip fully, thus forcing the knee to straighten and the heel to come into contact with the ground.

5.   During the course of the rotation, the hips move up and down. Tense the legs, especially at the knees and ankles. Ensure that the knee of the front leg does not move.

● *Turning the Hips—Repetitions*

Turn the hips repeatedly as though driving a screw into the ground. This movement is of primary importance in the advanced stages of karate. Consequently, this practice is of great value. The muscles used in turning must be strengthened by repeated practice until this action becomes second nature.

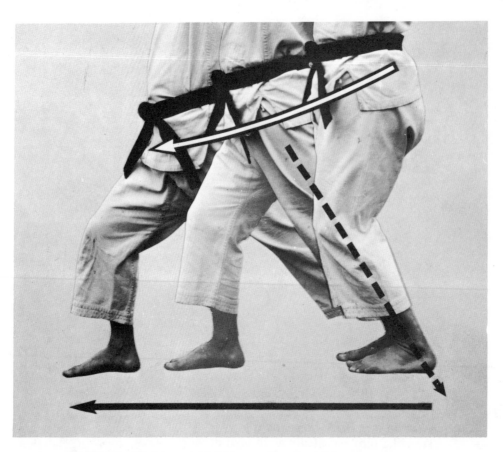

Pushing the hip forward. Left leg provides the driving power

Thrusting the Hips Forward

Thrusting the hips forward is also very important in karate. By thrusting the hips forward and at the same time taking a big step ahead, it is possible to deliver a strong attack. Also, after the delivery of a punch or kick, this forward movement affords the opportunity to follow up the initial attack quickly. A successful attack depends greatly on the powerful and speedy forward thrust of the hips. This particular movement is often used by advanced students in contests.

Thrusting the hips forward differs from merely stepping forward. Just as a jet plane is driven ahead by the thrust of its powerful jet engine, the body must be propelled forward. To accomplish this, move your weight forward onto one leg, and as the body and the other leg pass the supporting leg, thrust sharply backward with the supporting leg to propel the body forward.

From Informal Attention Stance, thrust hips to side

The body is pushed forward by the reaction which occurs when the supporting leg is straightened and thrust backward and downward against the ground. The speed with which the body moves forward is in direct proportion to the thrust of the supporting leg against the ground. The greater the reaction of the floor against the thrust of the leg, the faster the forward movement of the body.

Remember that thrusting the hips forward does not mean merely stepping forward, but rather moving out with the driving power of the supporting leg.

If the body leans forward slightly, the pushing power generated by the leg will be greater. The extent of the lean depends on such considerations as distance from the opponent and stance assumed. Avoid leaning forward to the point where the body is unbalanced.

If the hips are correctly thrust forward, power travels through the thrusting leg to the hips. From the hips it continues to the backbone, the shoulder, and through the arm to terminate ultimately in the fist. To transmit this power effectively from the hips to the arm, a tight connection must exist between the hips and the upper body. To achieve this connection, tense the muscles around the abdomen and the lower back. If the muscles are loose, only a part of the potential power will travel along the desired route and the punch will lose effectiveness.

To take a concrete example, it is obvious that an *oi-zuki* (lunge punch) depends for its effectiveness on the power generated by the forward thrust of the hips.

The hip thrusting principle which applies to forward movements also holds true of movements to the side and to the rear. If it is necessary to move quickly along a diagonal to the rear into the back stance, the hips must be thrust strongly to the rear. To do this, begin by moving one foot diagonally backward and then thrust strongly downward and forward with the other leg. This action will push the body diagonally backward.

Similarly, to move to the side into the straddle-leg stance, thrust sharply downward and sideways with one leg. The reaction will push the body to the opposite side.

Keep in mind that to move in any particular direction it is not enough just to step in that direction. It is necessary to thrust strongly with the supporting leg in the opposite direction from that you wish to take. The reaction propels the body in the desired direction. Repeated practice is necessary to attain proficiency.

From Informal Attention Stance, thrust hips to rear

From Informal Attention Stance, thrust hips forward

● *Thrusting the Hips Forward—Specific Points to Remember*
(Moving from the left-front stance to the right-front stance.)

1.   Begin by shifting the weight to the supporting leg and moving the center of gravity forward. Keep the knee of the supporting leg bent, but flexible. Tighten the muscles of the supporting leg.

2.   Draw the rear leg to the supporting leg as the body moves forward. Relax the muscles of the rear leg to facilitate a smooth forward movement.

3.   Keep the foot of the supporting leg in firm contact with the floor. Lift the opposite foot slightly and draw it forward to a position next to the foot of the supporting leg. The feet should touch slightly.

4.   Halfway through the forward movement thrust sharply backward and downward with the supporting leg at an angle of 45 degrees to the ground. This will drive the hips forward. At the same time advance the opposite foot one step. Keep the upper body perpendicular to the ground throughout this movement.

5.   Relax the moving leg during the forward movement, but at the instant of termination tense all the muscles involved. After an instant's tension the muscles relax again and the moving leg becomes the supporting leg for the next forward movement, or plays its role in some other action.

6.   When stepping forward the moving leg must swing in a half circle to the supporting foot and then out again. Move the foot smoothly and maintain continuous movement. Imagine that the thickness of a sheet of paper separates the foot from the ground.

7.   Be sure that the hips move along a plane parallel to the ground, with no fluctuation up or down. Also, prevent the hips from swaying from side to side during the movement. Any deviation from the horizontal plane will reduce the force of the forward thrust. (See illustrations)

8.   Flex the muscles of the lower abdomen throughout the movement, and keep the upper body perpendicular to the ground. The latter point is important to retain the ability to adjust to changing circumstances.

Maximum power cannot be obtained when hips bob or waver

Correct form

● *Thrusting the Hips Forward—Training Method 1*
(Informal attention stance to front stance)

1.   Assume the informal attention stance with the hands on the hips. Extend the elbows to the sides and press the thumbs of both hands against the back of the hipbones, forcing them upward. Relax the shoulders, tense the lower abdomen, and throw the chest out. Keep the knees flexible.

2.   To move into the left-front stance, move the body forward and thrust downward and backward with the right leg. At the same time, push the hips strongly forward with the thumbs.

3.   As the hips move forward, step ahead with the left foot, sliding it smoothly over the ground.

4.   Stop the left foot with the knee correctly bent. The body should now be in the front stance facing forward. (See sequence of photos above.)

5.   Withdraw the left foot to its original position and return to the informal attention stance.

6.   Practice moving from the informal attention stance to the right-front stance. (See sequence of photos on page 67.)

7.   Repeat these movements many times on both the left and right sides.

Movement of hips when moving forward from Informal Attention Stance ←

● *Points to Avoid*

  1. The thrust of the rear leg is weak and the body is pulled forward with the shoulders. (See photos below.) This impairs stability and results in ineffective techniques. Tighten the ankle of the rear leg and drive it strongly backward and downward.

  2. The heel of the rear foot is raised and the front foot bears too much weight during the forward movement. If the opponent sweeps your front foot with *deashibarai* (foot sweep), you will fall. Keep the heel of the thrusting foot pressed firmly against the ground.

  3. The foot of the moving leg steps forward in advance of the movement of the upper body. This prevents a coordinated movement of the body and contributes to an ineffective technique. Advance the hips as quickly as possible and attempt to coordinate the body's action. All parts of the body must come to a stop at the same instant. Note that if the front foot steps out in advance of the rest of the body, the opponent can easily apply a foot sweep, as in point 2 above.

Incorrect forms. Body leans too far forward

←

Movement of hips when moving from Front Stance

● *Thrusting the Hips Forward—Training Method 2*
(Left-front stance to right-front stance)

1. Assume the left-front stance at *hanmi* with the hands on the hips.

2. With the left leg supporting the weight, draw the hips and the right foot forward, keeping the upper body perpendicular to the ground.

3. At the halfway point of the forward movement, the left foot supports the weight, and the right foot is next to the left and parallel to it, lightly touching the ground. The right hip and shoulder are still slightly to the rear. (See illustration)

4. Pressing the hips forward, thrust sharply backward and downward with the left leg and step forward with the right. Assume right-front stance, facing forward.

5. Return the right foot to its original position and assume the left-front stance.

6. Repeat this action several times and then practice on the opposite side. After additional training in these movements, go continuously forward from the left-front stance to the right-front stance to the left-front stance, without returning to the original position as before.

● *Points to Avoid*

1. The supporting leg is not stable and the body is unsteady as it moves forward. If this occurs, the hips cannot be pushed forward strongly. Tighten the ankle and the knee of the supporting leg. However, retain some flexibility in the knee of the supporting leg.

2. The moving leg advances erratically. Relax the muscles of the moving leg to permit a light smooth forward movement.

3. When the hips advance, the upper body leans forward and does not remain perpendicular to the ground. Press the hips strongly forward with the thumbs.

H. Ochi (right) deflects Y. Tabata's kick and delivers a right punch to the mid-section in the finals of the 1966 All-Japan Karate Championship Tournament at the Budokan. Ochi won by decision.

Chapter 3

Balance and Center of Gravity

Balance plays an important role in all sports. Good balance depends on stability. To achieve stability, stand firmly on both feet, make the area of the base produced by both feet as large as possible and keep the center of gravity near the center of this base. Powerful techniques can be performed under these conditions, provided, of course, that the other requirements necessary to strong techniques are met.

If the center of gravity falls near the outer limits of the base area, balance will be weakened. Should the center of gravity travel outside the base area, balance cannot be maintained and the body will fall.

Without correct balance, it is impossible to deliver powerful techniques. Moreover, the follow-up to the initial technique cannot be launched until balance is recovered, resulting in a slow attack. Defense against the opponent's attack is also difficult without proper balance.

Correct Balance

Stability is especially important in the case of foot techniques, because the base area is limited to the sole of the supporting foot. Furthermore, the whole body is in motion during a kick, creating a shift in the center of gravity. To maintain stability under these circumstances, fully utilize the spring-like shock- and movement-absorbing ability of the leg and the hips. In addition, fully bend the ankle of the supporting leg during the kick. The object should be to keep the center of gravity within the base area.

Kick and step back

←

Step diagonally forward and deliver kick 45 degrees to front

It is even more difficult, in terms of balance, to deliver a kick while the body moves from one position to another. Try to develop the ability to deliver a kick at the end of every movement. Your position must be stable enough so that balance remains, even though the body is supported only by one leg. If your position is unstable you cannot deliver an effective kick or instantly block and counter the opponent's attack. Practice until your body can maintain a position well enough balanced to permit the delivery of a powerful kick at any time.

Kicks are often delivered with the heel of the supporting foot raised. This situation further reduces the base area and produces an unstable position. To maintain balance under such circumstances requires great tension in the muscles of the abdomen and legs. This position, if continuously maintained, requires a good deal of energy to control the nerves and muscles, resulting in increased fatigue. Therefore, be sure to keep the entire sole of the foot in firm contact with the ground.

Because the body moves around attacking and defending, it is obvious that the center of gravity will often leave the base area. However, if the amount of deviation is fairly small, various sensitive organs and muscles will automatically react to return the body to a balanced position. This sensitivity is better developed in the case of the more skillful student, who can recover from a greater degree of deviation. In other words, he can regain his balance even if his center of gravity moves relatively far from its base area.

Lowering the center of gravity contributes to stability. However, if the knee of the supporting leg is excessively bent when delivering a kick, the kick

Move sideward and kick

**Step directly for-
ward and kick**

will lack sharpness and possess limited range. Never-theless, under certain circumstances it is useful to kick from a low position. For example, it is some-times possible to duck under an attack directed at the head and then to counter by kicking.

If the center of gravity moves even slightly off the base area toward the target during a front kick, the knee of the supporting leg will be forced too far forward and the heel will rise. The result will be an ineffective kick. Also, if you kick at a too distant target and then attempt to return the kicking foot to its original position, you may lose your balance and fall. To avoid these errors and to retain balance when kicking, shift the base area (the supporting foot) to accord with the new position of the center of gravity. Do this by returning the kicking foot to a position somewhere in front of the supporting foot instead of to its original place, then assuming the front stance or some similar stance. From this bal-anced position you are ready to apply subsequent techniques.

Step backward at 45 degrees and kick

73

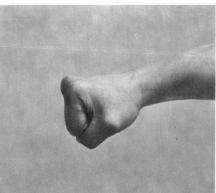

Chapter 4

Hands and Feet
Can Be Weapons

Strengthening the Hands and Feet

In karate many parts of the body serve as weapons. The hands, elbows, feet, and knees are most utilized, and they become effective and powerful weapons when strengthened through proper training and when employed in coordinated action with other parts of the body.

In Japanese fencing, training instills the idea that the sword is connected to the swordsman: that it is a part of his body. On the other hand, in karate no definite weapon is used. The body itself provides weapons which can be selected according to the situation.

However, this kind of multi-purpose weapon cannot deliver an effective attack unless it is strengthened and hardened. Without this training, the part of the body used as a weapon will be subject to injury.

Merely hardening the fist is useless. The fist can only serve as a strong weapon when supported by the power of the wrist, elbow, arm, and other parts of the body. However, systematic training of the hands and feet, coordinated with the supporting movements of the rest of the body, can forge devastating weapons.

The fist and *shutō* (knife-hand) of the skilled reflect power and beauty. These features are the result of the tightness and balance of the hand and the wrist. From the degree of harmonious interaction exhibited by the fist, wrist, and forearm, one can judge the relative skill of the karate student. It is said that powerful, well-controlled, and fine techniques start from well-trained wrists and ankles. They are an important factor in the production of power and speed, although this fact is often overlooked. Remember that the hands and feet are a starting point in karate.

Use of the Hands

The hand can be used both opened and closed.

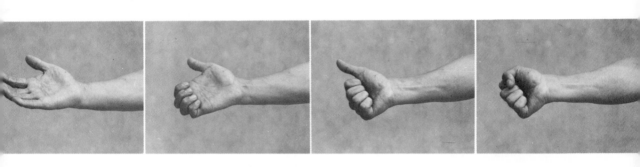

● *Making a Fist—1*

Fold the fingers inward at the middle joints. The tips should reach the base of the fingers. Continue bending the fingers inward until they are tightly pressed into the palm. Fold the thumb over the fingers and firmly press the index and middle fingers with the thumb. In forming a fist in this way the little finger tends to become weak and relaxed. Take care to prevent this from occurring. (See photos.)

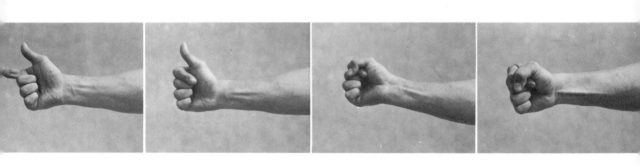

● *Making a Fist—2*

Bend the middle, ring, and small fingers inward until they are tightly pressed into the palm. Then fold the index over the middle finger, pressing the latter downward. The index finger should be at a slight angle to the middle finger. Fold the thumb over the index finger and press downward. (See photos.)

This method of making a fist was widely used until about 30 years ago, but few karateists employ it today. It declined in popularity because, although the index and middle fingers form a tight ball, the little finger tends to be quite loose. Also, it is initially somewhat difficult to make a fist in this way. However, if one becomes accustomed to this method, the fist can be quickly formed. Both methods of making a fist are useful and will result in effective techniques.

Types of Fists

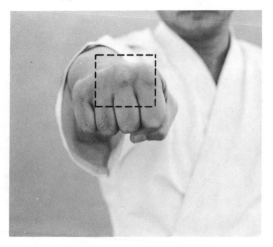

Seiken (fore-fist)

● *Seiken* (*fore-fist*)

Seiken is usually employed to deliver a thrust punch (*tsuki*). The part of the fist which hits the target is that area from slightly above the middle joint to the knuckle of the index and middle fingers. At the moment of impact all the power in the body must flow through the arm in a straight line and terminate in the fist. Tense the wrist and insure that the wrist and the top of the fist form a straight line. If the wrist is bent, power will not be transmitted to the fist, and the wrist may be injured. Because *seiken* is employed more often than any other kind of fist in karate, training in its use must be thorough and complete.

● *Uraken* (*back-fist*)

In *uraken* the fist is formed as in *seiken*. The part of the fist used to strike, however, is the back of the hand and the tops of the knuckles of the index and middle fingers. *Uraken* is used chiefly to attack the opponent's face and the side of his body. Deliver this strike with a snapping motion of the forearm.

Uraken (back-fist)

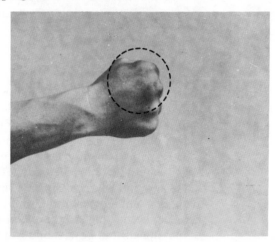

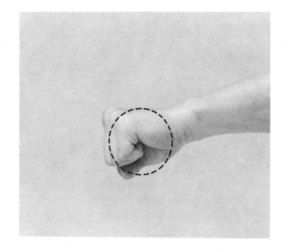

Kentsui (fist-hammer)

● *Kentsui* (*fist-hammer*)

Kentsui is also called *shutsui* (hand-hammer) or *tettsui* (iron hammer). After forming the fist as in *seiken*, use the bottom of the fist to strike the target. As with *uraken*, make use of the snap of the forearm to deliver the attack.

● *Ippon-ken* (*one-knuckle fist*)

Form the fist as in *seiken* but allow the middle joint of the index finger to protrude. The thumb, instead of being folded over the index and middle fingers, presses the side of the index finger to strengthen it. This fist is used to attack the bridge of the nose, the point below the nose, and between the ribs.

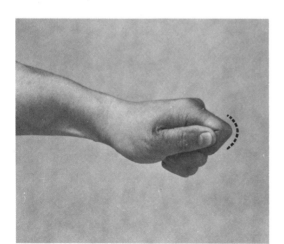

Ippon-ken (one-knuckle fist)

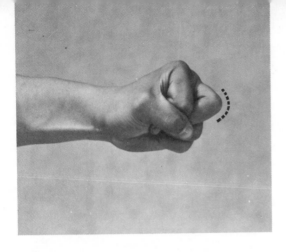

**Nakadaka-ken
(middle-finger knuckle fist)**

● *Nakadaka-ken (middle-finger knuckle fist) or Nakadaka-Ippon-ken (middle-finger one-knuckle fist)*

Form the fist as in *seiken*, but allow the middle joint of the middle finger to protrude. Fold the thumb over the index and middle fingers. Squeeze the middle finger tightly with the index and ring fingers to provide support, and press the thumb down on the index and middle fingers. The middle-finger knuckle fist is used for the same purpose as the one-knuckle fist.

● *Hiraken (fore-knuckle fist)*

Bend the fingers inward until the tips just touch the palm. Allow the fingers to bend only slightly downward at the knuckles. Press the thumb tightly against the index finger, or fold it back into the palm. This fist is often used to attack the point under the nose, or between the ribs.

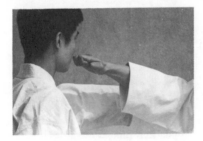

Hiraken (fore-knuckle fist)

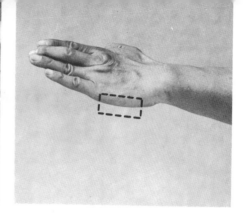

Shutō (knife-hand)

Open-Hand Strikes

● *Forming Kaishō (open-hand)*
Do not merely hold the hand open to form *kaishō*, but press the fingers tightly together. Bend the thumb at the joint and press it against the side of the palm. As in *seiken* the wrist and the back of the hand must form a straight line. Tense the wrist tightly. Do not depress the thumb too much at the base.

● *Using Kaishō*
Shutō (knife-hand)—When the open hand is used for *shutō*, power must flow into the fingers until the fingers are tensed and strong. This applies especially to the small finger. Imagine that power is flowing into the fingers and then outward from the outer edge of the palm. Use this outer surface of the hand like a knife or sword to strike the opponent's arms or legs as he attacks. It is also effectively used in attacks to the opponent's temple, the side of his neck, or his ribs. When applying the knife-hand, snap the forearm outward from the elbow joint with maximum speed and power.

Haitō (ridge-hand)—In *haitō* employ the opposite side of the hand from that used in the knife-hand. The striking area extends from slightly below the base of the index finger to the first joint of the thumb. The ridge-hand can be used in the same way as the knife-hand.

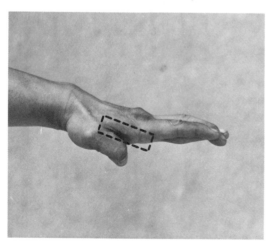

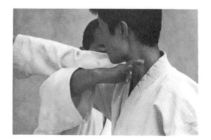
Haitō (ridge-hand)

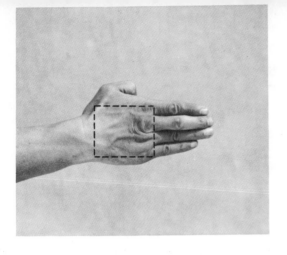

Haishu (back-hand)

Haishu (*back-hand*)—Use the entire surface of the back of the hand to strike in *haishu*. The back-hand is mainly employed for blocking. However, a strike to the side of the opponent's body or to his solar plexus with the back-hand will produce a strong effect.

Nukite (*spear-hand*)—In *nukite*, the tips of the first three fingers form a fairly level surface, necessitating a slight bend in the middle finger. In the preceding methods of forming *kaishō* (open-hand), the fingers were kept straight. The tips of the fingers in *nukite* are used to attack the solar plexus, the point between the eyes, the armpit, and other areas susceptible to attack with this weapon.

When the spear-hand is formed with the tips of only two fingers, either the middle and index, or the thumb and index, it is called *nihon-nukite* (two-finger spear-hand).

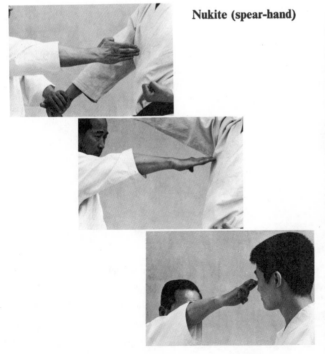

Nukite (spear-hand)

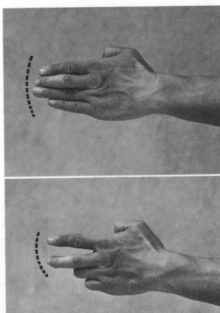

Teishō (palm-heel)

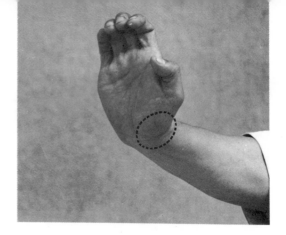

● *Special Uses of Kaishō (open-hand)*

Teishō (*palm-heel*)—Bend the hand upward at the wrist, and flex the wrist. Use *teishō* to brush the opponent's attacking arm sideward or downward. It is also very powerful when used to attack the opponent's chin.

Seiryūtō (*ox-jaw hand*)—Bend the hand sideways at the wrist so that the edge of the hand and its extension into the wrist form a curve. Force the edge of the hand forward to maintain this position. Use the ox-jaw hand to block a forward thrusting attack and to attack the opponent's face and collarbone.

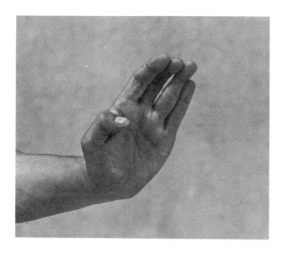

Seiryūtō (ox-jaw hand)

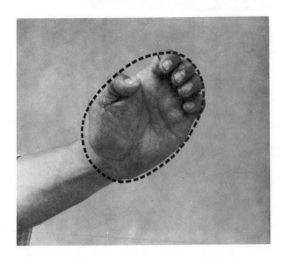

Kumade (bear-hand)

Kumade (*bear-hand*)—Form *kumade* by bending the fingers at the middle joint until the tips of the fingers just touch the palm. Bend the thumb and press it against the side of the palm. Stretch the palm fully and use all of its surface to attack. Use the bear-hand to attack the face with either a direct forward thrust or a sweeping sideward motion.

Kakutō (*bent-wrist*)—Bend the hand downward to its maximum extent and use that part of the wrist which forms the bend as the striking surface. Use the bent-wrist to attack the opponent's punching arm or his armpit with a snapping motion of the forearm.

Kakutō (bent-wrist)

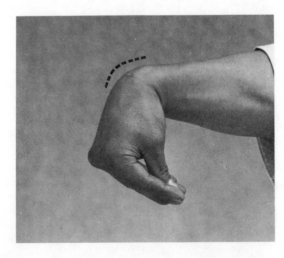

Keitō (chicken-head wrist)

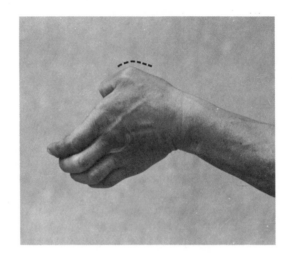

Keitō (*chicken-head wrist*)—Bend the hand in the opposite direction from the ox-jaw hand and flex the fingers and the thumb slightly inward. The striking area will be the base and first joint of the thumb. Attack the opponent's punching arm or his armpit with a snap of the forearm.

Washide (*eagle-hand*)—Press the fingertips together until the fingers resemble a bird's beak. The eagle-hand is useful in attacks against the throat and other vital points.

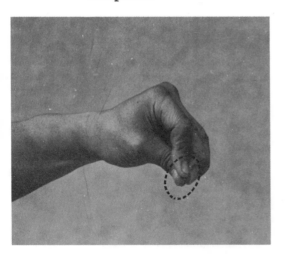

Washide (eagle-hand)

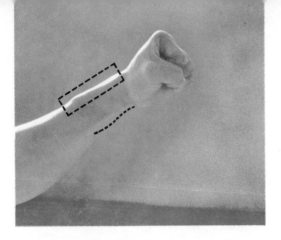

Wan (arm)

Wan (arm)—This area of the forearm is also known as *wantō* (arm-sword), and *shubō* (arm-stick). The arm is used mainly to block and to sweep aside the opponent's attacking arm or leg. If this part of the arm is toughened, it can administer a shock to the opponent's attacking arm or leg strong enough to discourage further attack. The part of the forearm on the side of the thumb is called *nai-wan* (inner arm), and the opposite side is *gai-wan* (outer arm). The upper surface of the forearm is called *hai-wan* (back arm), and the opposite side, or that above the palm, *shu-wan* (palm arm).

Empi (elbow)—(The term *empi* is used to describe the part of the arm used in this strike, and also the strike itself.) This is also known as *hiji* (elbow). This part of the arm can be used to deliver a powerful blow to any part of the opponent's body For example, the face, chest, or abdomen can be attacked with *empi*. This strike is especially effective when the opponent is standing very close. Even women and children can use *empi* with powerful effect against an assailant's attack. Elbow strikes are possible against an opponent standing at the front, the rear, or the side. The strike may travel upward, downward, and in a half circle, as well as in a straight line parallel to the ground. In performing these strikes, the section all around the tip of the elbow can be used, but the area actually selected will depend on the direction of the strike.

Empi (elbow)

Koshi (ball of the foot)

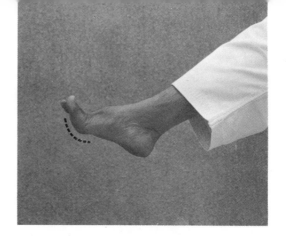

Use of the Feet
The foot can deliver a blow equal in power to that of the hand.

Koshi (*ball of the foot*)—This part of the foot is also known as *jōsokutei* (raised sole).

In karate, kicks are usually delivered with the ball of the foot as the striking surface. By curling the toes upward and using the ball of the foot it is possible to deliver kicks to the opponent's face, chest, abdomen, and groin. To kick effectively, raise the toes as much as possible, and tense the area around the toes and the ankle.

Sokutō (*foot edge*)—This part of the foot is used in kicks directed sideward. The edge of the foot on the side of the little toe serves as the striking area. In modern karate we curl the toes upward when kicking with the edge of the foot, but in the past the toes were curled downward. It is easier to tighten the foot in the latter method, but when the toes are curled upward the ankle enjoys greater flexibility. Either method can be used to good effect.

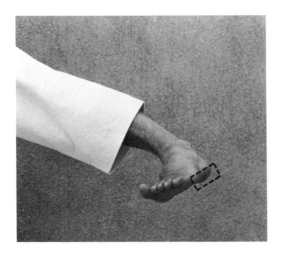

Sokutō (foot edge)

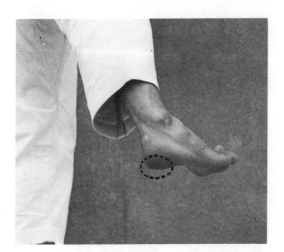

Kakato (heel)

Kakato (*heel*)—This area is also called *enshō* (round heel). This part of the foot is used in kicks directed backwards. A back kick is highly effective against an opponent attempting to grasp your body from the rear, or one who has secured an arm hold from the side or rear.

Haisoku (*instep*)—The area used in *haisoku* is the top of the foot from the toes to the ankle. The foot is stretched downward and the toes point downward. Use *haisoku* in kicks aimed at the groin.

Haisoku (instep)

Tsumasaki (tips of toes)

Tsumasaki (*tips of toes*)—Press the toes tightly together. The ends of the toes serve as the striking area. Can be used in kicks aimed at the groin or midsection.

Hizagashira (*knee*)—This area is also known as *shittsui* (knee hammer). As in the case of the elbow, use the knee in close infighting to attack the groin, the side of the body, and the thighs. Women and relatively weak persons can very effectively use the knee as a defensive technique.

Other areas useful for striking, such as the head, the forehead, and the shoulder have not been treated here. Remember that many areas of the body can serve to deliver offensive and defensive techniques. Study the construction of the body to discover additional possibilities.

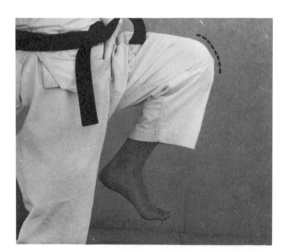

Hizagashira (knee)

Part II
Training in
Fundamental Techniques

H. Nishiyama sways back to avoid T. Okazaki's vicious kekomi and prepares for a right tsuki counterattack.

Chapter 5
Tsuki (Punching)/Theory and Practice

Tsuki—Delivery

● *Tsuki may be applied in the following ways:*

1. *Gyaku-zuki* (reverse punch)—Punch with the hand located on the side opposite to the forward leg.

2. *Oi-zuki* (lunge punch)—Punch with the hand located on the same side as the forward leg. *Oi-zuki* is effective when the opponent is some distance away.

3. *Ren-zuki* (alternate punching)—In either *gyaku-zuki* or *oi-zuki*, punch quickly two or three times with alternate hands.

4. *Dan-zuki* (consecutive punching)—Use the same hand to deliver two or three blows in rapid succession.

5. *Morote-zuki* (double-fist punch)—Punch with both hands at the same time. At the moment of impact the arms are either horizontally or vertically parallel to one another.

Tsuki (punching)—Variations

● *Tate-zuki* (*vertical-fist punch*)

Delivery: Twist the forearm inward a quarter-turn. The fist should be in a vertical position upon impact.

Kind of Fist: *Seiken* (fore-fist).

Route: Straight ahead.

Target: The face, the point under the nose, and the solar plexus.

● *Age-zuki* (*rising punch*)

Delivery: Punch from a lower to a higher plane.

Kind of Fist: *Seiken*, especially the first two knuckles.

Route: A half circle from the hip to the target.

Target: The opponent's face or chin.

● *Ura-zuki* (*close punch*)

Delivery: Twist the forearm a quarter-turn outward from a vertical fist position to one in which the inside of the wrist faces up.

Kind of Fist: *Seiken*. The back of the fist faces down upon impact.

Route: Straight and slightly upward.

Target: The face, solar plexus, and side of the body.

Flex the muscles of the back and side at the moment of impact, otherwise the close punch will be weak.

● *Mawashi-zuki*
(*roundhouse punch*)

Delivery: Rotate the hand almost a three-quarter turn from the hip to the target.

Kind of Fist: *Seiken*, with the thumb facing down at the moment of impact.

Route: A circular motion to the target. The circle described is somewhat larger than in the rising punch.

Target: The face, side of the face, and side of the body. Allow the elbow to brush the side until the last possible moment as the fist moves forward. Apply this punch with a twisting movement of the hip.

94

● *Kagi-zuki* (*hook punch*)

Delivery: Punch with the elbow bent at 90 degrees.

Kind of Fist: *Seiken.*

Route: To the side, at a right angle to the direction in which the body is facing.

Target: The side of the opponent's body or his solar plexus.

Step forward and to the side to deliver this punch. The muscles of the sides tend to relax at the moment of impact; flex these muscles when applying this punch.

● *Yama-zuki* (*wide U-punch*)

This punch is a variation of *awase-zuki* (U-punch).

Delivery: From *hanmi* (half-front-facing position), depress the leading shoulder slightly and punch with both hands, holding the forearms vertically parallel to one another. The back of the lower fist should face downward at the moment of impact.

Kind of Fist: *Seiken.*

Route: Direct the upper arm in a slightly curved arc upward and forward, as if tracing the rise of a hill to its summit. Thrust the lower arm directly forward.

Target: The face and the solar plexus simultaneously.

Keep the elbow of the upper arm slightly bent at the moment of impact. Keep the hip close to the lower elbow as a possible brace. Be sure both hands meet the target along the same vertical plane.

95

- *Awase-zuki* (*U-punch*)
  Awase-zuki is a kind of double-fist punch.
  Delivery: Use the upper arm as in the reverse punch. The lower arm acts as
             in the close punch with the back of the fist facing downward.
  Kind of Fist: *Seiken.*
  Route: Directly forward.
  Target: The face with the upper fist and the solar plexus with the lower.
           Hit the target with both hands simultaneously.

- *Heikō-zuki* (*parallel punch*)
  Heikō-zuki is also a kind of double-fist punch.
  Delivery: Punch directly forward with both hands, twisting the forearms
             inward a half-turn.
  Kind of Fist: *Seiken* or *naka-daka-ken* (middle-finger-knuckle fist).
  Route: Straight forward with both hands.
  Target: Ribs under the pectoral muscles.
           Attack simultaneously with both hands.

● *Hasami-zuki* (*scissors punch*)

Hasami-zuki is again a kind of double-fist punch.

Delivery: Use both hands at the same time, describing a half circle from the hips; first outward and then inward to the target.

Kind of Fist: *Seiken*, especially the first two knuckles.

Route: The hands describe a circle.

Target: Both sides of the body.

Keep the elbows close to the sides as long as possible when punching.

Fundamentals of Tsuki/Choku-zuki (Punch/straight punch)

Tsuki (punch) generally means *choku-zuki*. *Choku-zuki* is a thrust punch with *seiken* delivered at a target directly ahead. Turn the forearm inward 180 degrees and extend the arm as if it were a spear thrust forward from the side. This action will impart a powerful shock to the target.

Choku-zuki directed at the face is called *jōdan-choku-zuki* (upper straight punch), at the solar plexus area *chūdan-choku-zuki* (middle straight punch), and at the lower abdomen *gedan-choku-zuki* (lower straight punch).

Ideally, *choku-zuki* should be powerful enough to incapacitate the opponent, but this effectiveness cannot be developed in a day. Continuous daily practice over a relatively long period of time is necessary to forge *choku-zuki* into a strong weapon. But this practice must be properly done if it is to be effective. Therefore, the student must concentrate on the following points in training.

● *Route of Tsuki*

Tsuki will be ineffective unless it travels to the target over the correct route. The "correct" route in the case of the straight punch is a straight line from the starting position of the fist to the target. This can be done if you brush the inside of your elbow against your side during the course of the punch, and turn your forearm 180 degrees inward before you hit the target. These actions help to insure that the power potentiality in the punch does not go astray. If this power is transmitted on an unwavering line to the target, it will produce maximum shock upon impact.

● *Speed*

The formidable shocking power of karate techniques results from the momentum generated by the movement of various parts of the body, climaxed by a focus of these components at the instant of contact with the target. Speed is a major requirement in this operation. In fact, speed is of first importance from start to finish in the training in fundamental techniques.

As illustrated by the diagram on page 101, the movement of the body is, in general, operated by three components. Power is attained by speeding up the movement of each of these components. The faster the muscles are tensed, the more speed and, ultimately, the more power will be in the punch or kick.

To increase the speed of a punch, make use of the reaction of the opposite arm. The faster you retract the opposite arm, the more speed and power will be evident in your punch.

When the arm is stretched during the course of a punch, one group of arm muscles stretches while another contracts. Proper balance must prevail between these two muscle groups for a speedy and effective punch. If, for example, the muscles which must stretch are tensed, the arm movement will lack smoothness and the punch will be ineffective.

Beginners often use unnecessary muscles with the necessary ones. They must learn which muscles are essential for the performance of a particular movement and use only those. Effective techniques depend on the proper selection and use of the body's muscles.

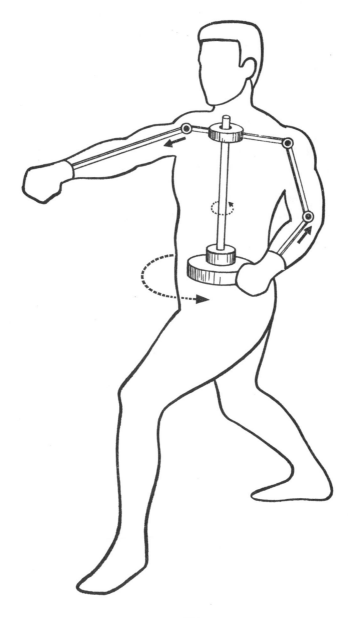

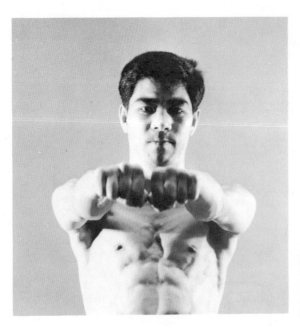

Learn to concentrate your power.
Raise both arms in front of the body
with the fists at the level of the
solar plexus. Alternately tense and
relax all the muscles of the body.

● *Concentration of Power*

Deliver a thrust punch by stretching the arm smoothly and rapidly toward the target. Release all unnecessary tension from the arm and hand at the start, but be sure to concentrate all the power of the body in the punching fist at the moment of impact. Make use of the reservoir of power stored in the hips as you begin your punch. This power flows through, and is increased by, the muscles of the chest, shoulder, upper arm and forearm. This principle also holds true in the case of a strike or a kick. Remember that an effective technique in karate is produced by a concentrated blast of power at the moment of impact.

The diagram and photos on this and the following pages illustrate the method of power concentration. Notice that the muscles at the front and side of the abdomen are strongly tensed, linking the chest and the hipbones firmly together. When the hips are properly set and the body is correctly supported by the thigh muscles, the standing position is firm and stable. This stable foundation enables the power of the hips to flow to the chest, shoulder, and arm. In the photos the arm muscles used in raising the arm and those which straighten the arm are strongly tensed, as are the forearm muscles. Note also that the muscles around the armpit are flexed to prevent a rebounding or flying backward of the arm and shoulder when the fist hits the target.

Power can be concentrated only when the hips, chest, shoulders, arms, wrists, and fists are firmly linked, and all necessary muscles function fully. If, during a thrust punch, the shoulder is raised or moved forward in advance of the movement of the body, you will be unable to tighten the muscles at the side of the chest fully. Even if the arm muscles are tensed, the reaction of the impact will cause your punch to rebound off the target.

Muscles Used in Tsuki (punching)

1. Biceps
2. Triceps
3. Deltoid
4. Teres major
5. Serratus anterior

6. Latissimus dorsi
7. Obliquus externus abdominis
8. Pectoralis major
9. Rectus abdominis

● *Training Method for Chūdan-choku-zuki* (*middle straight punch*)

1. Assume open leg stance of natural position, facing forward. Relax the shoulders and arms, and keep the hands at the sides.

2. Raise the left hand to the height of the solar plexus, palm open and down, and formed as if about to grasp something. Bring the right hand to the side above the hip and form a fist, drawing the elbow to the rear. It is very important in this position to draw the right hand back fully.

3. Withdraw the left hand to the side, closing the hand and forming a fist. It must take the same position above the left hip which the right hand had above the right hip. Simultaneously, drive the right hand forward at top speed along the most direct line to the target. Rotate the forearm so that the back of the fist faces up, and strike the target with *seiken*.

4. Open the right hand and relax. Assume the same position as before, but with the hands reversed. Repeat the movement in #3 above, punching with the left and withdrawing the right hand to its place above the hip. After practicing this movement, the student should be able to relax the body without opening the hand after each punch.

| Shoulder drop-ped too low | Shoulder raised | Shoulder thrust too far out |

● *Points to Remember*
1. Keep the upper body perpendicular to the ground. Do not lean forward.
2. Form *seiken* correctly and firmly.
3. Be sure the punch travels to the target along the most direct route.
4. When withdrawing the hand to the side, pull it back as if to hit the hip. Withdraw the hand with maximum speed.
5. Keep the shoulders relaxed and in a natural position. There is a tendency for the shoulders to rise or for one shoulder to move ahead of the other.
6. Tense the abdominal muscles properly.

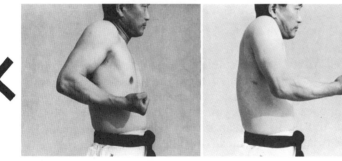  

If shoulder is raised, hand will travel an incorrect course to target

Keep shoulders relaxed, natural and steady during the movement

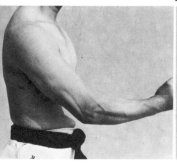 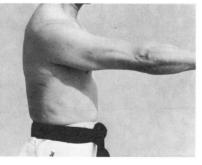

● *Gyaku-zuki* (*reverse punch*)

The reverse punch is delivered from a strong, stable stance, and can give a powerful shock to the target. Rotate the hips, keeping them at the same level during the turn. Straighten the rear leg and shift the center of gravity slightly forward. Imagine that you are pushing the hipbones forward as you turn. The blow will be ineffective if the center of gravity is too far to the rear at the finish of the movement.

This punch begins with the rotation of the hips. The power of this hip movement is transmitted to the chest, shoulder, arm, and fist, and culminates in a strong shock on the target. However, to prevent any loss of power, be sure the bodily reaction resulting from the impact of the fist on the target is supported in reverse order by the fist, arm, shoulder, chest, and hips. If the body is not tensed at the moment of impact, the consequent reaction will reduce impact power. Therefore, the hips, chest, shoulders, arms, and hands must form one solid mass at the moment of contact. To achieve this effect, all the muscles necessary for *gyaku-zuki* must work together harmoniously and tense powerfully at the same instant.

In conclusion, remember that the hips play a leading role in the performance of the reverse punch. Practice this punch and learn how the hip movement forms the basis for the movement of the upper body.

Starting position for Reverse Punch

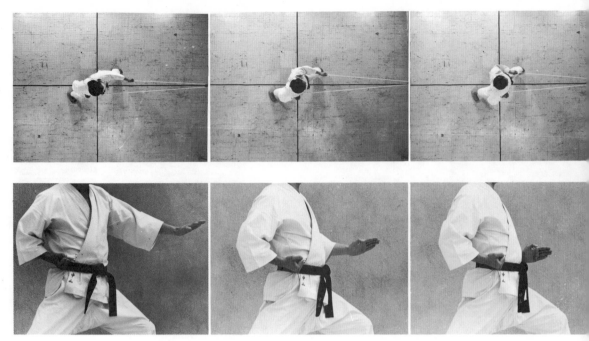

Fully withdraw left hand to side, and rotate hips

● *Important Considerations in Gyaku-zuki*

1. Lower the hips and assume a stable stance in either the front stance or the rooted stance.

2. Do not use the power of the arm and shoulder alone to deliver the punch, but concentrate instead on utilizing the power of the hips. Draw the left hand to the side, timing this motion to the rotation of the hips. During this movement, keep the right hand at the side. As illustrated in the series of photos above, imagine that the left hand and the right hip are connected by a rope attached to a pulley some distance ahead. As the left hand withdraws, the right hip should automatically move forward.

3. Deliver the punch, utilizing the reaction of the rear leg, which drives downward and backward against the ground. Be sure that the rear leg is fully straightened and flexed at the moment of impact.

The reaction caused by driving the rear leg into the ground generates power which travels upward through the leg and then is transmitted to the punch in a forward direction. (See the diagram on page 109). Theoretically, the smaller the angle formed by the rear leg and the ground, the greater will be the reaction and the more power can be transmitted to the fist. However, do not assume a position which is so low that it lacks flexibility.

**Straighten rear leg
and drive fist forward**

● *Training Method for Gyaku-zuki*

1.   Assume the left front stance at *hanmi*. Relax the upper body. Keep the knee of the rear leg slightly bent and flexible. Extend the left arm with the hand at the height of the solar plexus, palm downward and open as if to grasp something. Place the right fist at the side with the elbow drawn back. Face forward.

2.   Withdraw the left hand and simultaneously rotate the hips on a plane parallel with the ground. At the same time, straighten the knee of the rear leg, thrust the foot hard against the ground, and drive the right fist forward to the target.

3.   Return the right fist to its initial place above the hip, turning the hips clockwise, and resume the original position.

4.   Repeat this practice, alternating from the left-to the right-front stance.

Advancing while practicing Reverse Punch

Knee of rear leg is de pressed and heel raised

Right hip is left behind and upper body leans forward

Upper body leans to right

● *Points to Remember*

1. During the movement the hips tend to rise. Keep the hips down and the soles of the feet firmly on the ground.

2. When punching, the elbow of the striking arm is liable to leave the side, causing the hand to travel to the target over an incorrect route. Ensure that your elbow brushes lightly against your side as you punch.

3. The shoulder is liable to move in advance of the hip, reducing the amount of power transmitted to the punching arm by the hip rotation. Relax the shoulder and deliver the punch with the power generated by the turn of the hips alone.

4. Move the arms and the body in the following order. Remember that both hands move simultaneously.

> *Withdrawing Hand*
> Hand—Arm—Shoulder—Chest——HIPS——
> *Punching Hand*
> HIPS—Chest—Shoulder—Arm—Hand

5. At the moment of impact the shoulder on the punching side may have advanced too far ahead of the hip. Because of this excessive shoulder movement, the muscles of the side and back cannot be tensed, resulting in an ineffective technique.

6. The turn of the hips must be quick and sharp. The faster this can be performed, the better.

7. There is a tendency for the upper body to lean forward at the moment of impact. Avoid this incorrect position.

● *Effect of Stance on Attacking Range in Gyaku-zuki*
To extend the range of an attack, widen the distance between the feet and lower the hips. For example, an attack from the front stance with the hips relatively high and the feet only narrowly separated would achieve only a short range. An attempt to increase this range by leaning forward would result in loss of stability and an ineffective attack. Instead, widen the distance between the feet by stepping farther in the direction of the target with the front foot and lowering the hips.

Photos at left illustrate the effect on attacking range of changes in foot position and height of hips. Note that greater range is achieved by moving the front foot in the direction of the target while keeping the rear foot stationary.

If moving the front foot forward does not bring the target within range of the fist, do not lean forward to make up the remaining space. Instead, attack with the foot.

Move hips forward along same horizontal plane

● *Oi-zuki* (*lunge punch*)

Oi-zuki is a punch delivered at the end of a long forward step. In this movement the center of gravity undergoes a big shift. The forward momentum of the body gives additional force to the lunge punch, resulting in a more powerful blow than is possible by a reverse punch.

To perform the lunge punch, step forward with the rear foot from left-front stance to right-front stance. At the same time attack the face area or chest area with the *seiken* of the same side of the body as the advancing foot. For example, if you step forward with the right foot, attack with the right hand.

If you fail to step forward quickly, the opponent may anticipate your attack and apply a counter, or sweep your advancing foot and upset your balance. To prevent this, push the hips forward strongly by driving the supporting foot hard against the ground as you move ahead. (See page 109 for a discussion of this movement.) Do not raise the heel of the advancing foot, but slide the foot over the floor. Attempt to move forward as smoothly and rapidly as possible.

● *Important Considerations in Oi-zuki*

1. When advancing the rear foot, first draw it close to the supporting foot and then step outward and slightly to the side, describing a kind of semicircle. Slide the foot lightly over the floor as it moves forward.

2. As you begin your advance, move the hips forward until they are over the supporting leg. At this point the entire weight will be supported by one leg. As you continue to move forward, drive your supporting leg toward the ground and use the resulting reaction to propel your hips forward.

3. Keep your body at *hanmi* until the moment your entire weight rests on the supporting leg.

4. Drive your arm forward at the same instant as you begin to rotate your hips from *hanmi* to their terminal position. End the movement of the feet, hips, and arms simultaneously.

5. Attempt to convey to the punching arm every possible ounce of power generated by the reaction of the supporting leg against the floor.

6. In theory, loss of power is minimized when the upper body leans forward at an angle such that the supporting leg and the punching arm are permitted to thrust in opposite directions along the same plane. Considerations such as stability and the nature of the technique to follow prevent assuming this forward lean. However, lowering the hips as much as possible also keeps power loss to a minimum because at the moment of impact this action serves to reduce the size of the angle between the rear supporting leg and the floor, and produces greater power along the horizontal plane. Therefore, lower your hips to produce maximum power.

7. Be sure to thrust your hips in the same direction taken by your punch. In other words, move your center of gravity toward the target.

8. Make full use of the power created by the rotation and forward thrust of your hips.

9. During the course of the movement, prevent your body from bobbing up and down by moving your hips forward along a straight line parallel to the ground.

When hips and punch move in varying directions, the attack is weakened

• *Training Method for Oi-zuki—1*

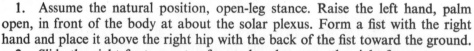

1. Assume the natural position, open-leg stance. Raise the left hand, palm open, in front of the body at about the solar plexus. Form a fist with the right hand and place it above the right hip with the back of the fist toward the ground.

2. Slide the right foot one step forward and assume the right-front stance.

3. As you slide forward, withdraw the left hand above the left hip, forming a fist with the back of the hand facing downward. Simultaneously, thrust the right fist forward, turning the forearm 180 degrees until the back of the fist faces up.

4. Withdraw the right foot and return to the original position.

5. Practice the foregoing movements on the opposite side, sliding the left foot one step forward to the left-front stance and punching with the left hand.

6. Return to the original position.

7. Practice these movements, alternating from side to side.

• *Important Considerations*

1. The forward movement of your foot must be smooth. Make it light and fast. Also, move forward quickly and smoothly to correspond with your step.

2. Do not lean forward or allow the shoulder to precede the body. Keep the upper body perpendicular to the ground and the hips and shoulders directed forward. Deliver the punch with the hip instead of with the shoulder or arm alone.

3. Straighten the knee of the rear leg, and flex the muscles of the leg, body, and arm at the moment of impact.

Do not raise or lower hips during movement

● *Training Method for Oi-zuki—2*

1. Assume the left-front stance in left downward block position at *hanmi* with the right fist above the right hip. (See starting position in photos.)

2. Take a big step forward with the right foot and assume right-front stance, facing forward.

3. As you step forward, withdraw the left fist to a position above the left hip and punch forward with the right, revolving the forearm inward 180 degrees.

4. Withdraw the right foot and return to the original position. Practice the foregoing movements repeatedly.

5. Practice the lunge punch on the opposite side, beginning in right-downward block position at *hanmi* and punching with the left hand.

6. Practice the lunge punch alternating from right to left.

● *Important Considerations*

1. The hips tend to rise when you bring the rear leg forward. Therefore, keep the knee of your supporting leg properly bent throughout the movement so that the hips advance along the same horizontal plane.

2. The body is liable to move forward at an angle to the direction of the punch. Several precautions can help prevent this situation. Be sure that throughout the punch the distance separating the feet does not exceed the width of the hips. Move the hips directly forward and do not allow the slight sidewise movement of the advancing foot to affect their direction. Also, aim hips and punching arm in the same direction. If all available power is not applied in the same direction, the effect of the punch will be lessened.

Jab, Reverse Punch and Jab

Jab and Lunge Punch

Flowing Punch

● *Nagashi-zuki* (*flowing punch*)

The flowing punch resembles the lunge punch, because the movement of the body gives added force to both punches. The flowing punch can be thrown from *hanmi* while stepping either forward or backward at a 45 degree angle. The punch is especially effective when blocking and delivering a counterattack in the same motion. Deliver the flowing punch by using the power generated by hip rotation as your body moves forward or backward at a 45 degree angle to the opponent.

● *Kizami-zuki (jab)*

The jab is also a kind of lunge punch. It is done by snapping the leading fist forward in a jab without moving the front leg, using hip rotation and the forward thrust of the rear leg to gain power. The jab can be a decisive punch, but it is usually employed to keep the opponent off balance and to set him up for a lunge punch, reverse punch, or some other strong attack. It is possible to deliver jabs without changing the position of your center of gravity. However, you can also change positions and move forward or backward. Whether or not the center of gravity changes, an effective jab relies on hip rotation and rear leg thrust for power.

● *Training Method for Kizami-zuki—1 (From jab to reverse punch)*

1. Assume a ready position with your left side forward.
2. Thrust downward and backward with the rear leg. Utilizing this reaction, push the hips forward and slide the leading foot forward a half-step.
3. As you move forward, deliver a decisive punch forward with the left hand while rotating the hips clockwise. The body should be turned 90 degrees to the right at the moment of impact.
4. Snap the left hand back to a position above the left hip. Simultaneously, rotate the hips counterclockwise, and—
5. Straighten the rear leg, driving the right hand forward in a reverse punch. The target is usually the face area for the jab and the chest area for the reverse punch.

● *Important Considerations*

1. There is a tendency when throwing a jab to withdraw the opposite hand slowly and to revolve the hips slowly. Withdraw the opposite hand hard to the side and snap the hips around.
2. Relax the knee of the rear leg immediately after applying a jab to prepare for a follow-up attack.
3. When executing the reverse punch after a jab, be sure to withdraw the left hand sharply as the right delivers the reverse punch. Also straighten the knee and thrust sharply downward and backward with the rear leg. Simultaneously, revolve the hips 90 degrees counterclockwise.

● *Training Method for Kizami-zuki—2 (From jab to lunge punch)*

1. Assume a ready position with your left side forward.
2. Slide the left foot a half-step forward and deliver a jab with the left hand.
3. Move your weight onto the left leg, changing the center of gravity.
4. Withdraw the left fist and at the same time take a long sliding step forward with the right foot.
5. Simultaneously, apply a lunge punch with the hand.

● *Important Considerations*

1. Keep the hips at an angle to the front (the right hip back) while the body weight shifts onto the left leg.
2. The upper body tends to lean forward when shifting from jab to lunge punch. To prevent this lean, push the hips forward as much as possible.
3. When shifting into a lunge punch bend the knee of the front leg properly, and relax the advancing leg to ensure a smooth forward movement.

Chapter 6

Uchi (Striking)/Theory and Practice

Striking Techniques

Elbow strikes cannot, strictly speaking, be called *uchi*, but for the sake of convenience they are included as a category of *uchi*. Elbow and knee strikes should be classified as *ate-waza* (smashing techniques). The elbow strike is known as *hiji-uchi* or *empi-uchi*. It is one of the most powerful attacks in karate, one which can be used effectively even by women and children as a self-defense measure against physically stronger attackers. The elbow strike is especially effective in close in-fighting or when the body is held from the back.

Uchi is a powerful technique when used as a single attack, but it is even more effective when used in combination with other techniques. For example, immediately after delivering a lunge punch to the opponent's face, strike the side of his face with the back-fist strike of the same hand, using the snap of the elbow and forearm. Another possibility is to attack the opponent's neck with the knife-hand strike from the outside and then, by instantly bending the forearm inward, to strike his solar plexus with the elbow.

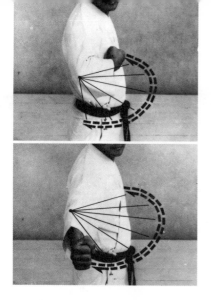

**Correct route of fist
in striking**

● *Elbow and Forearm Snap in Uchi*

The following points relating to the snap in *uchi* are very important.

1. Snap the forearm outward smoothly and rapidly, using the elbow as the center of movement. Relax the elbow. If the slightest elbow tension remains, the arm will act like a mechanical toy that needs oiling, and the technique will be ineffective.

2. Relax the shoulder and tighten the striking fist or open hand. If the shoulder is tense the arm may swing out without any snap.

3. Straighten the elbow fully as the hand is snapped outward. The more the arm is stretched at the elbow, the greater the effect of the strike.

4. Snap the hand outward with maximum speed. The strike must be fast to be effective.

5. Using the muscles which stretch the arm, snap the arm outward with great speed to its maximum extent. When the arm reaches this position, immediately relax the stretching muscles. At that point, the muscles which serve to withdraw the arm will automatically act to return the arm to its original position. This sudden withdrawal of the forearm completes the snap. To effectively snap the arm outward, learn how the muscles of the arm work to stretch and withdraw the forearm.

Back-fist Strike

Training method (1)

Training method (2)

Hammer-fist Strike

Striking Techniques Using the Fist
● *Uraken-uchi* (*back-fist strike*)
● *Kentsui-uchi* (*hammer-fist strike*)

With the elbow as the center, snap the forearm outward in a 180 degree circle. In the back-fist strike the back of the fist or the tops of the knuckles of the index and middle fingers are used to strike the target. This technique becomes more effective if the wrist as well as the elbow is snapped. However, at the beginning the snap of the elbow is of primary importance and should be thoroughly learned.

In the hammer-fist strike the bottom of the fist delivers the strike. It is mainly employed to strike the face, solar plexus, and side of the body.

Both back-fist strike and hammer-fist strike can be applied along either a horizontal or a vertical plane.

● *Important Considerations*

1.   Avoid striking with the entire arm. Utilize instead only the snap of the forearm from the elbow to develop a sharp and effective technique.

2.   In the case of a horizontal strike the forearm travels along a plane parallel to the ground. When delivering a strike along a vertical plane, the fist travels in a half circle from the chest upward and then downward again to the target.

3.   Point the elbow toward the target before striking to ensure that the fist travels directly to the target, instead of traveling a longer route.

● *Training Method for the Horizontal Strike—1*

1. Assume the natural position. Turn head to right. Place left fist in front of right hip and right fist at left side of chest.

2. Strongly withdraw the left hand to a position above the left hip and move the right elbow to the right side with the forearm and upper arm parallel to the ground.

3. As a continuation of the movement in #2, snap the right fist to the side and immediately withdraw it again to the position in #2.

4. Return to the position described in #1.

● *Training Method for the Horizontal Strike—2*

1. Assume the natural position.

2. Turn the head to the right. Place the hands in a position similar to that described in #1 above.

3. Sliding the right foot to the side, strongly withdraw the left hand to a position above the left hip and move the right elbow to the right side w th the forearm and upper arm parallel to the ground.

4. As a continuation of the movement in #3, assume the straddle-leg stance, snap the right fist to the side, and immediately return it again to the right front side of the chest.

5. Return to the natural position, withdrawing the right foot to its initial position.

Striking Techniques with the Elbow

● *Hiji-ate or Empi-uchi* (*elbow strike*)

The elbow strike differs somewhat from strikes utilizing the hand. It belongs to the category of *ate-waza* (smashing techniques) rather than to striking techniques.

The elbow strike is performed by driving the elbow forward, sideward, backward, upward, or downward. The elbow strike is most effective in situations where the free movement of the body is lost. For example, it serves as an effective defensive technique when an opponent holds your wrist or your arm.

● *Important Considerations*

1. The elbow strike is effective when used to counterattack at short range, but tends to lose its value as the distance from the opponent increases.

2. When applying the elbow strike keep the upper body perpendicular to the ground. Move the hip in the direction of the strike. If the upper body is not kept perpendicular to the ground, the technique will be weak.

3. Keep the fist and forearm of the striking arm as close to the body as possible, brushing the side of the body at the start of the technique.

4. Rotate the forearm anywhere from 90 to 180 degrees to gain greater striking power. Place the forearm initially in such a position that this rotation is possible.

5. Relax the shoulders. To increase the impact, bend the elbow fully and tense the arm muscles just before striking the target.

- *Mae-Hiji-ate or Mae-Empi-uchi (forward elbow strike)*

Use forward elbow strike to attack the opponent's chest or abdomen when he is directly ahead. This strike is especially effective when standing face to face with an opponent who has grasped your wrist or jacket.

- *Training Method for Elbow Strike*

   1.   Assume the left-front stance at *hanmi.*

   2.   Place the left hand in front of the body, and the right fist above the right hip with the back of the fist facing downward.

   3.   In one coordinated action withdraw the left fist to a position above the left hip, thrust the right hip forward, and drive the right elbow in a half circle toward the target. Rotate the right forearm 180 degrees counterclockwise as you drive the elbow forward.

   4.   At the conclusion of this movement the upper body faces forward and the top surface of the forearm is up. Be sure to twist the forearm inward as much as possible.

   5.   Return to the position in #2, withdrawing the right hip. This movement can be practiced from right- as well as left-front stance. It is also necessary to practice the forward elbow strike when shifting from natural position to front stance.

- *Important Considerations*

Keep the right fist close to the body as you apply the forward elbow strike. Its correct path is from the right hip to the left side of the chest. Brush the right forearm along the side of the body as you bring the elbow forward.

Forward Elbow Strike

Side Elbow Strike

● *Yoko-Hiji-ate or Yoko-Empi-uchi* (*side elbow strike*)
Use the side elbow strike to attack the opponent's chest or abdomen. This technique is especially useful against targets at your side. For example, it can be readily employed to counterattack an opponent who attempts to grab from the side, or to counterattack one who has attacked from the front and is moving to the side.

● *Training Method for Side Elbow Strike*
1.   Assume the straddle-leg stance.
2.   Face to the right. Place the left fist, with back of the fist facing up, in front of the right hip. Place the right fist in front of the left side of the chest with back of the fist facing down.
3.   Begin to move the left fist toward the left hip and at the same time thrust the right elbow toward the right side, rotating the forearm inward.
4.   Continue the movement begun in #3 and bring the left fist to a position above the left hip with back of the fist facing down. Complete the elbow strike to the right side by extending the elbow fully to the side with the right fist in front of the chest, and back of the fist facing up.
5.   Return to the position in #2.

Practice these movements alternately on both sides. It is also useful to practice the above movements from the natural position, assuming the straddle-leg stance as the elbow strike is completed. Keep the right forearm close to the chest during its movement to the side. It should lightly brush the chest during its course.

• *Ushiro-Hiji-ate or Ushiro-Empi-uchi* (*back elbow strike*)

Use back elbow strike to strike the chest or solar plexus of an opponent who attacks from the rear. It is especially effective against an opponent who attempts to hold from the rear.

1.   Assume the left-front stance, with the upper body facing forward.

2.   Place the left fist over the left hip and extend the right hand forward as if the reverse punch had just been completed.

3.   Look to the rear, pull the right hip to the rear, push the left fist forward, and drive the right elbow to the rear, rotating the forearm outward 180 degrees until the back of the hand faces down. Pull the right shoulder to the rear as the elbow is driven backward.

4.   Complete the movement in #3 by propelling the elbow strongly backward and ending in *hanmi*.

5.   Move the right hip forward and return to the position in #2.

Practice the above movement alternately on both sides.

Additional practice consists of applying the back elbow strike while stepping backward with one foot from natural into front stance or back stance.

• *Important Considerations*

The rearward movement of the elbow is similar to that in the straight punch. Draw it back as strongly as possible, and be sure that the fist ends up at the side of the body.

● *Yoko-Mawashi-Hiji-ate or Yoko-Mawashi-Empi-uchi* (*side-round elbow strike*) Use the side-round elbow strike to attack the side of the face or chest of an opponent standing directly in front of you. Also, after evading the opponent's frontal attack and stepping diagonally to the side, use this strike as a counterattack.

● *Training Method for Side-Round Elbow Strike*

1. Assume the left-front stance at *hanmi*.

2. Extend the left fist forward and place the right fist at the side approximately as in the downward block.

3. Pull the left hand to the left side, push the right hip forward, and move the right forearm forward so that the right hand ends in front of the right side of the chest and the elbow describes a large half circle. Rotate the right forearm 180 degrees inward during this movement.

4. Complete the movement in #3 by drawing the left hand fully to the left side, turning the body so it faces forward, and striking the target with the elbow.

5. Pull the right hip back and return to the position in #2.

Practice this technique alternately on both sides. Also, practice this elbow strike by starting from the natural position and then moving into the front stance.

● *Important Considerations*

Move the elbow of the striking arm in a large half circle at the same time the right hip is rotated.

● *Tate-Hiji-ate or Tate-Empi-uchi* (*upward elbow strike*)

Use the upward elbow strike to attack the chin or solar plexus of an opponent directly ahead. This elbow strike is extremely effective when delivered from a low position attained by moving into and under the opponent's attacking arm.

● *Training Method for Upward Elbow Strike*

1.   Assume the right-front stance with the body facing forward.

2.   Extend the open left hand in front of the body at about the height of the solar plexus with the back of the hand facing up. Place the right fist above the right hip with the back of the fist facing down.

3.   Withdraw the left hand to a position above the left hip, rotate the hips counterclockwise, and bring the right elbow forward and upward in a half circle.

4.   Simultaneously, complete the withdrawal of the left fist, turn the upper body to the left at a 45 degree angle to the front, and finish the strong upward thrust of the right elbow. End the movement of the right fist beside the right ear.

5.   Rotate the hips clockwise and return to the position in #2.

Practice this movement alternately on both sides. Also, practice the upward elbow strike by moving from the natural position to the front stance.

● *Important Considerations*

1.   Keep the forearm close to the side as it travels upward. Coordinate the upward movement with the rotation of the hips.

2.   Rotate the hips along a plane parallel to the ground so that the upper body remains perpendicular to the ground.

3.   Tighten the buttocks as if to push them upward. Do this in addition to rotating the hips and the strike will be more powerful.

● *Otoshi-Hiji-ate* or *Otoshi-Empi-uchi* (*downward elbow strike*)

Use the downward elbow strike to attack the face, back of the head, or the body when these targets are in a relatively low position. A downward strike with the elbow is particularly effective after you block the opponent's attack and force him to bend forward, or after he falls.

● *Training Method for Downward Elbow Strike*

1. Assume the rooted stance with the left foot forward.
2. Place the left fist in front of the left hip, and raise the right arm above your head. (See illustration.)
3. Withdraw the left hand to the left side, lower the hips, and drive the right elbow downward, rotating the forearm counterclockwise until the back of the hand faces outward.
4. Complete the movement in #3 by withdrawing the left hand fully to the side, bending the knees deeply, lowering the hips, and striking strongly downward with the right elbow.
5. Straighten the knees and return to the position in #2. Practice this movement alternately on both sides.

● *Important Considerations*

Students tend to lean forward and lose their balance, striking the target with the arm only. Use the weight of the body to strike by dropping the hips and keeping the forearm perpendicular to the ground.

Training method   (2)

● *Training Method for the Vertical Strike—1*

1.   Assume the natural position. Turn your head to the right. Place your left fist in front of your right hip and your right fist in front of the left side of the chest. The backs of both fists must face up.

2.   Begin sliding your right foot to the side, withdraw your left fist toward the left hip, and begin an upward movement with the right fist, ensuring that it moves close to the chin.

3.   Complete the movements begun in #2 by fully assuming the straddle-leg stance, fully withdrawing the left hand to a position above the left hip, and snapping the right fist outward to the target. Be sure the fist moves along a vertical plane and is immediately snapped back to its initial position after striking the target.

4.   Return to the position in #1.

● *Training Method for the Vertical Strike—2*

1.   Assume the natural stance.

2.   Raise the left hand, either open or in a fist, to the left side of the head. Place the right fist in front of the navel, with the back of the fist facing the body.

3.   Take a long step forward with the right foot. Simultaneously, move the left fist toward the left hip and snap the right fist up and outward in a half circle, almost brushing the chest and the chin.

4.   Complete the movements begun in #3 by assuming the right-front stance, fully withdrawing the left fist to a position above the left hip, and snapping the right fist forward to the target. Withdraw the right hand again in a reflex motion as soon as it meets the target.

5.   Return to the natural stance by stepping back with the right foot.

● *Important Considerations*

1.   Relax the elbow of the striking arm in order to strike sharply and powerfully.

2.   Keep the striking fist tightly clenched and firm.

Before practicing the vertical strike with a forward or sideward step, practice the arm movements alone while standing in *shizen-tai*.

132

Shutō-uchi (knife-hand strike)
The knife-hand strike is performed in a similar
manner to the back-fist strike. However, in contrast
to the latter, the knife-hand strike employs the edge
of the open hand to strike. Use this technique to
attack the temple, the side of the neck, and the side
of the body. It can be delivered in two ways. For
example, when using the right hand to strike, the
hand can move either from left to right (from inside
outward), or from right to left (from outside inward).
● *Important Considerations*
　1.　Correct hip rotation is of primary importance.
When striking from inside outward, rotate the hips
in the opposite direction of the strike. On the other
hand, when striking from the outside inward, rotate
the hips in the same direction as the strike. The diagram below helps to illustrate this point. Unless
the hip movement precedes the hand movement, the
effect of the strike will be weak.
　2.　To achieve maximum power, rotate the striking hand a full 180 degrees from its initial position
to the target.

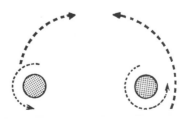

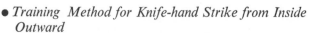

● *Training Method for Knife-hand Strike from Inside Outward*

1. Assume the right-front stance with the upper body facing forward.

2. Extend the left hand in front of the body at solar plexus height with the palm downward. Place the right hand beside the left ear with the back of the hand facing outward.

3. Withdraw the left hand toward the left hip and form a fist, rotate the hips counterclockwise, and snap the right hand outward from the left ear, turning the forearm.

4. Complete the movement begun in #3 by rotating the hips until the body is in the right-front stance at *hanmi*. Fully withdraw the left hand to a position above the left hip, and complete the strike outward with the edge of the right hand. At the moment of impact the palm of the right hand must face downward.

5. Return to the position in #2 by rotating the hips clockwise.

Repeat the above practice on both sides of the body.

After attaining some degree of familiarity with the above movements, practice the knife-hand strike while moving from the natural position to the front stance or the straddle-leg stance.

● *Training Method for Knife-hand Strike from Outside Inward*

1. Assume the left-front stance at *hanmi*.

2. Extend the left hand in front of the body at solar plexus height with the palm downward. Place the right hand at the side of the right ear with the palm facing outward.

3. Withdraw the left hand toward the left hip and form a fist, rotate the hips counterclockwise, and snap the right hand forward toward the target in a circle from the outside inward.

4. Complete the movement begun in #3 by rotating the hips counterclockwise until the upper body faces forward. Fully withdraw the left fist to a position above the left hip and complete the snap of the right hand to the target, turning the forearm 180 degrees. At the moment of impact the palm of the right hand faces upward.

5. Return to the position in #2 by rotating the hips counterclockwise.

Practice this movement on both sides of the body.

As in training for the knife-hand strike from the inside outward, practice it from the outside inward by moving from the natural stance to the front stance or the straddle-leg stance.

● *Important Considerations*

1. Stretch the hand until the palm is flat, and press the fingers together. Keep the wrist firm to ensure a strong snap. Relax the elbow to provide speed in the movement.

2. When applying the knife-hand strike, move the withdrawing hand with maximum speed. This procedure increases the speed and strength of the striking hand.

The author (left) follows up with a left yoko-geri attack as Y. Yaguchi, instructor, starts to withdraw his foot after a yoko-geri attempt.

Chapter 7

Keri (Kicking)/Theory and Practice

Keri includes some of the most powerful techniques in karate.
Keri is peculiar to karate and includes variations absent from other martial arts and sports. If sufficiently mastered, kicking techniques can have a more powerful effect than attacks with the hands. However, mastering kicking techniques requires much time and effort.

When kicking, good balance is of primary importance because the body weight is supported by only one leg. This situation is aggravated at the instant the foot hits the target by the strong counter shock of the kick. To counteract this shock, place the supporting foot firmly on the ground and fully tighten the ankle of the supporting leg. Attempt to absorb the shock with the ankle, knee, and hip of the supporting leg, and keep the upper body well balanced and perpendicular to the ground.

To achieve maximum effect, kick with the whole body instead of with the leg alone. Pushing the hips forward during the kick helps achieve this goal.

Be sure to withdraw your kicking foot quickly after completing the kick. This prevents the opponent from catching it or from sweeping your supporting leg. As soon as the foot is withdrawn it must be ready for the next attack.

Focusing Mae-geri (front kick)—Front View

The photo above clearly shows the condition of the muscles of the kicking leg at the instant the foot strikes the target. Note that the muscles at the back of the thigh, which usually serve to bend the leg, are fully stretched. These muscles are ready to contract rapidly as soon as those which extend the leg are relaxed. The lower leg will then instantly snap back to its original position.

Focusing Mae-geri (front kick)—Side View

This photo shows the muscles of the front and the inside of the thigh at the instant of focus. These muscles serve to extend the leg, and are fully tensed at the moment of impact.

The degree of power possible in a kick like the front kick is determined by the distance over which the foot travels, the speed with which it is driven, and the amount of snap imparted by the leg muscles. Note that the muscles at the inside of the thigh, those of the hip, and those at the front of the thigh are all strongly flexed at the same instant.

Keri (kicking)—Factors Involved

Bend the knee of the kicking leg to its maximum extent.

Begin by raising the knee of the kicking leg as high as possible and bending the knee fully. This action is an important preliminary to kicking, comparable to the run before the takeoff in broad or high jumping. Practice in lifting the knee also helps accustom the body to balancing on one leg, and aids in learning the first part of the correct course of a kicking foot.

Lifting and fully bending the knee of the kicking leg requires first the use of the hip muscles, and then those of the thigh. Because these muscles have some connection with the hipbones, the hips must be firmly stabilized to allow the muscles to operate fully. However, it is difficult to stabilize the hips unless the muscles of the abdomen are strong. Therefore, a strong abdominal region is necessary for powerful kicks.

Part of the reason for bending the knee fully is to keep the weight of the kicking leg as close as possible to the trunk. The kick has greater power if the leg is initially close to the body. By bending the knee fully, better leverage is obtained to make a quick and powerful kick.

During the kick, keep the supporting leg steady, with the knee slightly bent. If the knee is bent too much in an effort to keep the hips low, the muscles of the leg will support the body with difficulty. The knee and ankle will be loose, and it will be difficult to kick effectively. Be sure to bend the knee only slightly, lean the leg slightly forward, tense the muscles of the leg, and keep the sole of the foot firmly in contact with the ground.

Front Kick   **Side Kick**   **Round Kick**

Important Points in Raising and Bending the Knee
● *Mae-geri* (*front kick*)

1.   Raise the knee, keeping the sole of the foot parallel to the ground, but with the ball of the foot slightly higher than the heel.

2.   Keep the shin almost perpendicular to the ground.

3.   Pull back the heel as much as possible. A plumb line dropped from the knee should hit a point at the tips of the toes.

4.   Point the knee and the toes in the same direction.

5.   Turn the toes up and tighten the ankle.

6.   Relax the knee joint and keep it flexible, ready for the next movement.

● *Yoko-geri* (*side kick*)

The method of raising and bending the knee in the side kick is almost the same as that of the front kick. The following points, however, relate specifically to the side kick.

1.   When raising the knee, brush the foot lightly against the inside of the calf of the supporting leg. End the movement with the sole of the foot against the inside of the knee of the supporting leg.

2.   Extend the knee at about a 45 degree angle to the side at the height of the lower abdomen.

3.   Point the toes of the foot forward and direct the edge of the foot downward and parallel to the floor.

● *Mawashi-geri* (*round kick*)

1.   Keeping the body at *hanmi* raise the knee to the height of the abdomen, and raise the foot at the side close to the hips, with the toes pointing to the side and the sole facing the rear.

2.   Raise the leg so that the thigh and the lower leg are parallel to the floor at the same height.

3.   Bend the knee fully so that the heel almost touches the hip.

● *Important Points for the Supporting Leg in All Kicks*

1.   Ensure that a plumb line dropped from the buttocks falls just behind the heel. The center of gravity should be located somewhere between the toes and the heel of the foot.

2.   Keep all of the sole of the foot in contact with the ground.

3.   Bend the knee slightly and flex the ankle and knee joints.

4.   Ensure that a plumb line dropped from the front of the knee falls at the tips of the toes.

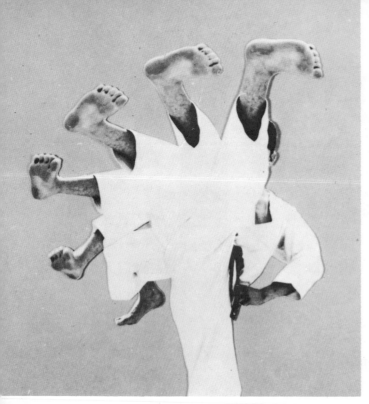

Round Kick

Learn the Principles behind the Snap Kick and the Thrust Kick.

There are two ways of kicking. The first is done with a snapping and, in most kicks, an upward movement of the foot. The second, by straightening the knee and thrusting the foot outward and often downward while stepping toward the target.

● *Keage* (*snap kick*)

Deliver the snap kick with a strong snapping motion, beginning from the raised and bent knee position of the leg described above. The foot describes almost a half circle during the kick.

In the snap kick, balance is often poor because of the restricted base provided by the supporting foot, and because the power of the kick is usually directed upward. Return as quickly as possible to a somewhat wider stance, with both feet on the ground. Maximum speed is essential in the execution of the snap kick, or, for that matter, any kick. A slow snap kick not only fails to create a powerful attack on the target, but results in an unbalanced position.

It has been said that the speedy withdrawal of the foot after it meets the target is more important than the initial outward movement. This does not mean that the outward movement should be slow. Deliver the kick with as much speed as you can, and make the withdrawal, if possible, even faster. A quick withdrawal prevents the opponent from grasping your leg, and allows an immediate return to a more stable position, ready for the following movement.

To deliver the snap kick, raise and fully bend the knee and then quickly and powerfully tense the muscles at the front of the thigh. This tension drives the foot outward. When the leg is fully extended, relax the muscles at the front of the thigh and tense those at the back. This action withdraws the foot.

The kick from beginning to end is very smooth, and there is no noticeable pause at the moment of impact. This is because the muscles at the back of the thigh are stretched as the leg is extended outward. A sudden release of tension in the front thigh muscles will immediately cause those at the back to contract, automatically withdrawing the foot. (Concerning this point, see the photos and explanations on page 137.)

Front Kick　　　　　　　　　**Side Snap Kick**

● *Important Points in Snap Kicking*

1.　If you are too intent on kicking, the knee joint of the kicking leg will tense, preventing a smooth movement. Relax the knee, raise the toes, and tense the foot.

2.　After kicking the target, withdraw the foot fully to a position beside the knee of the supporting leg.

3.　Concentrate all your power at the ball or the outer edge of the foot (depending on the kick) at the moment of impact. At the same time, push the hips in the direction of the kick.

Side Thrust Kick

● *Kekomi* (*thrust kick*)

From the raised and bent knee positions described above, a thrust kick can be aimed directly ahead or directly to the side. It can hit a target located at knee height, at waist height, or higher.

As in the case of a straight punch with the hand, be sure the foot travels the most direct course to the target. Keep the movement light and fast at the start of the kick, but concentrate maximum power in the foot at the moment of impact.

Most students prefer *yoko-geri-kekomi* (side thrust kick) to *yoko-geri-keage* (side snap kick), because the former is easier to learn, and there is a satisfying snap of the karate suit at the end of the thrust. However, the thrust kick is more difficult than it appears to be. You must correctly judge the distance separating you from your opponent, or your kick will fail.

Thus, a successful thrust kick depends upon correct distancing and split second timing. The foot must hit the target at the moment the leg is fully extended and exerting maximum power. If the foot hits the target too soon or too late, the resulting reaction will push the foot back toward the kicker instead of striking the target. This negative reaction is greatest when the foot hits the target with the leg already fully extended but improperly focused. This adverse reaction is more likely to destroy your balance when you kick waist high than when you kick at a downward angle. Remember the importance of distancing and timing in *kekomi*.

● *Important Points in Kekomi*

   1.   Flex the ankle and knee of the supporting leg.

   2.   Lean the upper body as much as possible in the direction of the kick. If you lean away from the kick, you will lose your balance. At worst, you will be propelled away from the target at the moment of impact.

   3.   Utilize the hips. Push them in the direction of the kick.

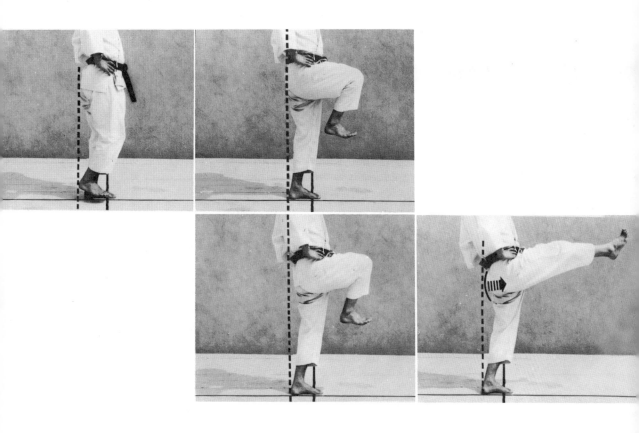

Learn to Use the Hips and the Ankles

An effective kick cannot be applied with the power of the leg alone. This rule holds true for the snap kick as well as the thrust kick. To kick effectively, add a springing motion of the hips to the power of the leg. Push the hips toward the target as the leg drives out and immediately withdraw them again as the leg is retracted. The ankle of the supporting leg must act like a spring to absorb the movement of the hips as well as the shock of the kick. Moreover, the supporting ankle must act to keep the sole of the foot flat on the ground throughout the kick. If part of the foot is raised, the supporting base is reduced and balance and stability are adversely affected.

The ankle of the supporting leg plays an important part in all kicking techniques. A strong, flexible ankle enables the hips to move smoothly and effectively. The supporting knee, for its part, must be kept immobile to provide proper balance.

Front Kick to body

Front Kick to face

Learn the Various Kicks

● *Mae-geri* (*front kick*)

Use the front kick to attack a target in front with the ball of the foot, the toes, or the instep.

● *Ushiro-ashi-geri* (*rear-leg kick*)

In this kick, use the ball of the foot of the rear leg to attack the target. The foot describes a half circle from its position close to the knee of the supporting leg to the target. This kick can effectively attack almost any part of the opponent's body, including the face, chin, chest, abdomen, groin, and thighs. The ends of the toes, tightly pressed together, can be used in the same way as the ball of the foot. However, if the toes are unaccustomed to this practice it can be rather painful. The instep can also be used, but it is usually ineffective except for attacking the groin or the chin.

● *Points to Remember*

1. Your hips tend to rise when you snap kick with the rear leg. Therefore, do not straighten the knee of the supporting leg, and keep the hips on the same horizontal plane throughout the kick.

2. If your hips remain behind and your upper body leans forward during the kick, the range of the kick will be reduced and its effectiveness correspondingly lowered. Therefore, move the hips forward as quickly as possible at the start, and maintain good balance with the supporting leg.

3. If the upper body is unbalanced, it is impossible to kick effectively. Therefore, tighten the muscles of the lower abdomen to maintain a tight connection between the upper and lower parts of the body.

4. After kicking, the next position of the kicking foot on the ground varies. However, in almost all cases, this foot must first return to a position close to the the knee of the supporting leg to expedite its movement onto the ground. An exception occurs when the kicking foot is not withdrawn, but slides down the opponent's body to the ground as either hand continues the attack. In general, the next position of the kicking foot depends on distance from the opponent, posture, and on the nature of the following techniques.

5. Keep the heel of the supporting foot firmly on the ground. If the heel rises, balance will be momentarily weakened, increasing the time necessary to shift to the next movement.

6. Ensure that the foot takes the shortest and straightest course in its route to the target. The rear-leg kick is most effective when the target is directly ahead.

● *Training Method for Rear-Leg Kick*

1. Assume the left-front stance with the fists at the sides. In the case of beginners it is better to place the hands on the hips.

2. Without moving the supporting foot, and keeping the knee bent, move the hips forward until the weight is entirely supported by the left leg. Simultaneously, raise and bend the knee of the kicking leg so that the foot moves past the knee of the supporting leg.

3. Continue the movement in #2 by snapping the·right foot back to the target.

4. Immediately, or reflexively, snap the foot back to a position next to the knee of the supporting leg.

5. Continue the movement begun in #4 and return to the position in #1. Repeat the above practice alternately on both sides of the body.

Note difference when hips are thrust forward (above) and when upper body leans forward (below).

● *Important Considerations*

1. Push the hips forward when kicking. If the hips are permitted to remain behind, the upper body will lean too far forward and bring the face within range of the opponent's attack. (See photos above.)

2. Keep the hips low to increase stability. However, if they are too low, the knee of the supporting leg will sink during the kick, reducing stability and shortening the kicking range. Bend the knee of the supporting leg enough to allow a plumb line from the knee to fall at a point just at the tips of the toes.

3. When kicking, point the knee of the supporting leg in the direction of the target. Failure to do this causes the kicking foot to stray from the target, and prevents the concentration of maximum power at the moment of impact. Ensure that the knee of the supporting leg is flexed and that it and the toes of the supporting foot point directly at the target.

Kicking foot sways to right and misses target

● *Mae-ashi-geri (front-leg kick)*
In the front-leg kick, the ball or the instep of the front leg is usually used to kick the target.

The method of kicking is similar to that for the rear-leg kick. However, in the front-leg kick the center of gravity remains to the rear of center during the kick. To kick, raise the knee of the front leg and bend it fully until the heel is as close as possible to the buttocks. From this position snap the foot outward to the target.

The front-leg kick, because of the comparatively smaller circle described by the kicking foot, lacks the power of the rear-leg kick. However, it is a very useful technique in certain situations. For example, while maintaining your position you can effectively counter an opponent as he moves toward you to attack.

The front-leg kick can also be applied from the front stance. For instance, after attacking with and missing a lunge punch, you can deliver an immediate kick to the body with the front leg. This technique is rather difficult, however, because the center of gravity is slightly forward of center in the front stance. To kick from this position means that the weight must be supported for an instant by the rear leg alone. Because the center of gravity is forward, it is difficult to maintain balance during this kick. Consequently, this technique is best practiced by more advanced karate students.

A karate student must be freely able to use either his front or rear leg to kick, depending on the requirements of the situation. His body must learn how to respond to changing circumstances. He must be instantly and almost unconsciously aware of changes in the position of his center of gravity, his stance, his distance from the opponent, and the location of the target.

● *Kekomi* (*thrust kick*)

The thrust kick is done by driving the ball of the foot or the heel against the opponent's solar plexus, groin, thigh, or knee. From the raised position of the kicking leg, strongly straighten the knee and thrust outward toward the target. This kick is especially effective when the target is in a relatively low position and your foot can travel diagonally downward. Kicking too high tends to upset your balance.

● *Important Points*

1. Use your hips as well as your leg to kick.

2. Lock out the knee of the kicking leg fully and powerfully to prevent the reaction of the impact from pushing the leg back toward you.

3. When you kick with the ball of your foot, tighten and straighten the ankle. However, when you use the heel, bend the ankle fully and push the heel forward.

4. Begin your thrust kick by raising the knee of the kicking leg as high as possible and by bending it fully.

5. *Kekomi* is similar to *keage* (snap kick) in other respects.

● *Training Method for Thrust Kick*

1. Shift weight to left leg and raise right leg, bending the knee fully.

2. Lock out the right knee quickly and powerfully, and aim your thrust kick at the opponent's midsection or groin. As you kick, keep your supporting foot firmly in position on the ground.

3. Withdraw your left foot to the position described in #1. Repeat thrust kicks alternately, using first the right and then the left leg to kick.

● *Special Considerations*

1. Thrust the hips forward as you kick. Imagine that you are kicking with the hips as well as with the leg.

2. In the thrust kick the upper body tends to lean backward. Except for special occasions, counter this tendency by carrying the center of the body well forward as you kick.

● *Body Position in Mae-geri* (*front kick*)

In photo A, the center of gravity falls within the base area of the supporting foot. This condition contributes to good balance. There is little chance here to add the forward momentum of the body to the strength of the kick.

A large upward snapping kick is possible from this position, and it enables you to meet the opponent's counterattack, or to deal adequately with any other change in the situation.

Although, in photo B, the center of gravity falls outside the base area of the supporting foot, good balance is still possible. Forward body momentum can strengthen your kick. The foot can easily snap outward and upward toward the target. Moreover, the kicking range is extended.

After kicking the target, you can place the kicking foot on the ground in front of the supporting foot, thereby easily maintaining your balance. If necessary, it is also possible to return the kicking foot to its initial position on the ground without upsetting your balance.

As in A, you can easily cope with the opponent's counterattack, or adjust to any change in the situation. In C, the center of gravity falls rather far outside the supporting base area. This situation makes for poor balance. The driving power of the body can be utilized here, but because the hips are behind the shoulders, it will be difficult to impart a powerful snap to the kick.

After kicking, you must set your foot down in front of the supporting foot. There is no chance to withdraw the foot and to resume your initial position.

Because the body leans forward, it will prove difficult to deal with the opponent's attack. A kick from this position generally gives the opponent an opportunity to attack your face with a punch.

● *Yoko-geri (side kick)*

This kick is usually directed to the side without turning the body. *Sokutō* (foot edge) is used to attack the target. The side kick can also be employed against a target directly ahead by turning the hips and body a quarter-turn left or right. Depending upon the opponent's position and other circumstances, you can kick to good effect with either a snap kick or a thrust kick.

● *Keage (snap kick) or Kebanashi (kickoff)*

The side snap kick is a snap kick using the foot edge against an opponent to the side. It is possible to kick the opponent's attacking arm from underneath upward, or to kick his groin, the side of his chest, his armpit, or his chin.

● *Important Points*

1. During the kick, point the foot and the knee of the supporting leg directly forward and avoid any change in their position. Keep the entire sole of the supporting foot in contact with the ground. Slightly bend the knee of the supporting leg and keep the supporting foot steady.

2. Raise the kicking foot to the knee of the supporting leg. Brush the inside of the supporting leg with the sole of the foot as it comes up. Point the knee of the kicking leg diagonally to the side at hip height, and point the foot straight ahead. Rotate your foot downward until the foot edge is directed toward the ground and is parallel to it.

3. Because you are kicking to the side, it is easy to lose your balance if your upper body leans too much away from the kick. When kicking, move the upper body in the direction of the target.

4. Withdraw your kicking foot to its original place as quickly as possible and resume a stabilized position. This action also helps prepare for the next movement.

5. Deliver this kick by snapping your foot upward in a semicircle. The knee serves as the pivot of the movement. When the target is relatively high, further elevate the knee of the kicking leg.

- *Training Method for Side Snap Kick*
  1. Assume the informal attention stance.
  2. Shift your weight to the left leg. Raise your right foot to the knee of the supporting leg, brushing the inside of the supporting leg with the sole of your foot on the way up. At this point the sole of the right (kicking) foot lightly touches the inside of the left (supporting) knee, and the right knee points 45 degrees to the side.
  3. Snap your foot directly to the side and kick the target with the foot edge.
  4. Snap your foot back to the position described in #2.
  5. Return to the informal attention stance. Practice snap kicks alternately on the left and right sides.

- *Special Considerations*
  1. If your hips move to the rear and your body leans forward, a common fault in the snap kick, you will be unable to kick directly to the side. Instead, you will kick slightly forward of the desired direction. A kick from this position loses some of its effectiveness. Prevent this fault by pushing your hips forward.
  2. If you fail to tighten the kicking foot, you will be unable to kick effectively with the foot edge. Fully tighten and bend your ankle, and push your heel in the direction of the kick.
  3. If the heel or either side of your supporting foot rises off the ground during the kick, you will lose your balance. Position the knee of the supporting leg so that a plumb line dropped from it will hit at the tips of the toes. Keep the supporting knee and the ankle firm and steady.
  4. Avoid twisting or excessively leaning the upper body in any direction during the kick. An erect and well-balanced position contributes toward a powerful kick and provides a solid base for the next movement.

● *Kekomi* (*thrust kick*)

From the raised knee position from which a snap kick is delivered, it is also possible to apply a thrust kick by thrusting the leg outward to the side. As in a snap kick, use the foot edge to kick the target. Employ the thrust kick to attack the solar plexus, chest, side, or the thigh of an opponent standing to your side.

● *Important Points*

1. When kicking, strongly lock out the knee of the kicking leg as you thrust to the side, until the thigh and lower leg form one unbroken line. The sudden and complete locking out of the knee guarantees maximum power in thrust kicks.

2. It is possible in thrust kick to raise the kicking leg as in the snap kick, with the knee directed somewhat to the side. However, a more effective kick results if you raise the knee in front of the chest as in the front kick. The foot travels a longer distance to the target from this latter position, generating greater power.

3. The thrust kick is strongest when your foot edge hits the target at a 90 degree angle.

4. Withdraw the kicking foot as nearly as possible along the same route it traveled to the target.

5. The suggestions concerning the use of the supporting leg in snap kicks apply also to thrust kicks.

- *Training Method for Side Thrust Kick*
  1. Assume the informal attention stance.
  2. Shift your weight to the left leg and raise the right leg high in front of the chest, bending the knee fully. In this ready position, the kicking foot points straight ahead, and the sole of the foot is directed downward parallel to the ground.
  3. Move the knee to the side and lock it out with a powerful thrust. At the end of the thrust your foot edge should hit the target with explosive force.
  4. After locking out for an instant, withdraw your foot and return to the position described in #2.
  5. Return to the informal attention stance. Repeat thrust kicks alternately on both sides of the body.

- *Special Considerations*
  1. Avoid kicking the target with the toes or with the sole instead of with the foot edge. Fully bend and tighten your ankle. Revolve your foot downward to the side and tighten it. As you kick, twist your foot inward as though you were trying to kick with the heel. By so doing you will ensure that all the surface along the edge of the foot will hit the target. Point the knee of the kicking leg forward throughout the kick.
  2. It is important to lock the knee of the kicking leg completely. Maximum power can only be obtained when the knee locks completely and the leg extends fully.
  3. In addition to the above, those special considerations outlined for snap kicks apply also to the thrust kick.

Fumikiri (cutting kick)

Fumikiri is a kind of side thrust kick. It is used to attack the opponent's leg or instep. Thrust your foot downward to the side and kick the target with the foot edge. Imagine that your foot is a cleaver or an ax head cutting into the target. The cutting kick is effective against an opponent standing in front or behind you, as well as against one at the side.

Fumikomi (stamping kick)

Fumikomi is very effective when directed against the opponent's knee or instep. To increase kicking power, shift your weight onto the kicking leg as you stamp downward.

Use the stamping kick and the cutting kick to escape from an opponent who has thrown his arms around you from the rear. These kicks also serve as preliminary feints to some decisive attack.

Instructor H. Nishiyama, All-American Karate Federation, Los Angeles, counters with gedan-kekomi (right) as Instructor T. Okazaki, AAKF, Philadelphia, attacks with jōdan-kekomi.

Mawashi-geri (round kick)

Use the round kick to attack an opponent directly ahead with the ball of the foot or the instep. Either the front or rear leg can deliver the kick. Swing the foot around your body in a large circle as you attack, rotating the hips. Kick with a snap of the foot, driving it from the outside inward. Maintain the kicking leg parallel to the floor at the moment of impact.

The round kick can convey a strong shock to the opponent's face, neck (or neck artery), chest, or abdomen. It is also possible to deliver this kick from the inside outward, instead of in the usual way. However, this technique is more difficult and is recommended only for advanced students.

● *Important Points*

1.   Do not kick with the power of the leg alone. Instead, propel the foot toward the target with the quick, strong rotation of the hips. When you kick with the right leg, your left foot, leg, and hip, your chest, and your head must all rotate in a counter-clockwise direction, while the knee and foot-drive forward toward the target.

2.   When you rotate the hips, the supporting foot is forced to turn in the direction of rotation. However, be sure the foot remains firmly in contact with the ground, and that it moves as little as possible.

3.   Exert pressure to push the hip upward on the side of the supporting leg. Force this hip upward throughout the kick to help tense the muscles of the abdomen and hip. Without this tension, balance will be impaired and smooth hip rotation difficult. When the hip is correctly forced upward, the opposite side of the abdomen should feel pressure.

4.   The round kick is most effective when the ball of the foot hits the target with maximum speed at a 90 degree angle. Therefore, rotate the knee, shin, and foot of the kicking leg around the body along the same horizontal plane parallel to the ground.

● *Training Method for Round Kick*

1. Assume the left-front stance at *hanmi* with fists in the ready position. Beginners should place the hands on the hips.

2. Maintain the *hanmi* position with the upper body and shift your weight onto the left leg. As your weight shifts, raise the right knee upward to the side with a fast, light motion, and raise the foot until the knee, lower leg, and foot lie along the same horizontal plane parallel to the ground. Bend the knee of the kicking leg fully and draw the heel as close as possible to the back of the right thigh. At this point the toes of the kicking foot should point directly to the side, and the sole should face the rear.

3. Rotate the hips counterclockwise and snap the foot outward and around toward the target. The kicking foot should describe a large circle around the body in its path to the target.

4. Return the hips and the kicking foot to the position described in #2.

5. Return to the position in #1.

Repeat this practice on alternate sides, first the right leg and then the left.

● *Special Considerations*

1. When you raise the kicking leg at the side, the upper body tends to lean forward or to the side. The smooth rotation of the hips is impossible under these conditions and your kick will be weak. Be sure to keep the body as upright as possible by pushing the hip of the supporting leg upward and forward, and by throwing the chest out.

2. Bring the fully bent knee of the kicking leg up high to about the waist, and the heel close to the rear, to make the arc of the kick as long as possible for a powerful kick.

3. The round kick will be ineffective unless the kick is correctly timed to the rotation of the hips. Keep the body at *hanmi* until the kicking leg is in position and the hips are ready to begin their rotation. Abandon the *hanmi* position only as the hips begin to rotate and the kick is propelled forward.

4. Leaning your body to the rear as you kick impairs balance and hinders the return to the starting position. Prevent this situation by tensing the muscles of the abdomen to keep the connection tight between the upper body and the kicking leg.

5. The round kick is a powerful attack, but it is easy to lose your balance after the kick. For example, if the hips rotate too far with the kick, it is difficult to return to the starting position quickly and your back will be exposed to the opponent's attack. Therefore, avoid rotating the hips too far. Advanced students sometimes use *renzoku-waza* (combination techniques) in this situation, shifting from the round directly to the back kick, as extensive rotation of the hips is necessary for this combination of kicks.

6. At the moment of impact, the knee of the supporting leg tends to straighten and the heel to rise. Tense the knee and ankle of the supporting leg to keep the knee bent and the foot flat on the ground.

Gyaku-mawashi-geri (reverse round kick)

While the ordinary round kick is a kick which travels to the target in a semi-circle around the body from the outside inward, *gyaku-mawashi-geri* does the reverse. In the reverse round kick the foot begins at the front of the body and describes a half circle outward to the target. Similar principles underlie the operation of both kicks. Use the supporting leg as a pivot, rotate the hips in the direction of the kick, and snap the foot toward the target.

If you try to kick too high, the heel of the supporting foot will rise and your kick will be weak. Aim your attack no higher than the opponent's solar plexus.

This kick should be practiced only by more advanced students.

Mikazuki-geri (crescent kick)

When an opponent attempts to attack with a punch, block his forearm as he steps close and counterattack with the crescent kick to his abdomen or groin. In this instance, kick with the ball of the foot. The crescent kick is sometimes used as a block. For example, when the opponent attempts a punch to your body, kick his forearm to the side as he attacks. Use the sole of the foot to apply this block.

● *Important Points*

The course the kicking foot travels is shorter in the crescent kick than in the round kick. Another difference is that in the crescent kick it is unnecessary to raise the leg to the side before kicking. The kick can be delivered directly from the original position on the ground. It follows, then, that compared with the round kick, the crescent kick is less powerful, but lends itself better to a surprise attack.

● *Training Method for Crescent Kick*

As in practicing the round kick, training for the crescent kick is usually done by kicking a target in front while standing in the front stance. However, practice can also consist of attacking a target at the side while in the straddle-leg stance. In learning to kick from the latter stance, do the following:

1. Assume the straddle-leg stance. Extend the left hand to the side, palm facing forward.

2. Transfer your weight to the left foot and simultaneously bring your right foot up and kick the left hand with the sole. The foot describes a crescent from the ground to the hand.

3. Return the foot to its original position over the same route it traveled to the target.

Practice alternately on both sides.

Instructor Y. Takahashi (right) counters Instructor M. Itaya's tsuki with a sokutō-keage.

Ushiro-geri (back kick)

Ushiro-geri is a kick directed against a target to the rear with the heel of either foot. The kick can be delivered with either a powerful thrust or with a snap. It is also possible to deliver a surprise back kick to the front by pivoting around, turning your back to the target, and propelling your foot outward. The back kick is especially effective against an opponent who has caught hold of you from the rear or who is attacking from the rear.

The back kick can be used to attack the opponent's solar plexus, abdomen, groin, thigh, and lower leg. It is often employed by advanced students as a follow-up to, or in combination with, the round kick.

● *Important Points*

1. Because it is difficult to kick accurately with a back kick, be sure your body is in the correct position before kicking. Aim your hip directly at the target. If your body is correctly lined up with the target, there is less chance of missing.

2. Correct balance constitutes a problem in the back kick. If your supporting leg does not provide enough stability, you may be thrown off balance by the reaction of the kick as it hits the target. Avoid excessive forward lean with the upper body as you kick. Tense the abdominal muscles and throw out the chest to maintain a strong connection between the upper and lower parts of the body.

3. Use the spring-like power in the hips to thrust the kicking leg backwards.

4. Bring the muscles of the buttocks into play to make your kick more powerful.

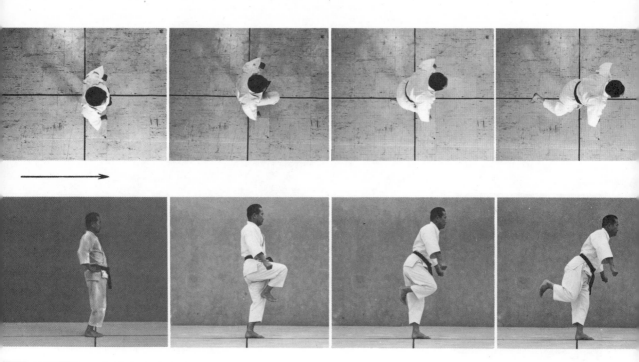

• *Training Method for Back Kick*

1.   Assume the informal attention stance or the front stance.

2.   Shift your weight to the left foot and raise the right knee high in front of the body as in the front kick.

3.   Lean your body slightly forward and in the same motion straighten your knee and thrust your foot toward the target behind you. If the target is close it is also possible to attack with an upward snap of the heel.

4.   After kicking the target, immediately return the kicking leg to the position in #2, and then to that in #1.

• *Special Considerations*

1.   The position of the supporting leg in the back kick should correspond to that in the front kick.

2.   When kicking, bend the kicking foot upward to its maximum extent, reducing the angle formed by the instep and the shin to the minimum. Aim the heel of the kicking foot directly at the target. The toes should point at a 45 degree angle toward the ground at the moment of impact.

3.   Even if the target is directly behind the hips, it is possible to miss. This failure is usually caused by not having the kicking leg project straight backwards. The knee of the kicking leg should slightly brush the knee of the supporting leg when shot backwards.

Instructor H. Kanazawa (England) jumps in the air for a tobi-yoko-geri as Instructor K. Enoeda (England) attacks with oi-zuki.

Tobi-keri (jump kick)

Tobi-keri is a powerful technique that must be performed with a certain boldness. You must leap high into the air and kick the target at the peak of your leap. The jump kick includes two basic methods of kicking. In one, push off with the front foot and kick with the rear foot. In the other, push off with the rear foot and kick with the front. The underlying principle is to execute the front kick while leaping.

One variation of *tobi-keri* is *nidan-geri* (double jump kick), a technique composed of two quick front kicks in succession during the course of a leap. The first kick, directed at the abdomen, is a short, sharp one; the second, aimed at the head, is a larger, more destructive attack. The target for both kicks should be located directly ahead.

Another variation of the jump kick is *tobi-yoko-geri* (jumping side kick), or *kesa-geri* (diagonal kick). In this technique deliver a side kick while the body is in the air. Leap high and deliver a thrust kick with the foot edge at a downward angle. Aim the kick at some point along the opponent's side anywhere from the head down.

● *Important Points*

1. Practice the jump kick only after attaining proficiency in ordinary kicks like the front kick, side kick, and *renzoku-geri* (combination kick). Jump low at first. Gradually increase your height as your skill increases.

2. The initial takeoff determines the ultimate height of your leap. Therefore, the ankle, knee, and hip joints must work as a strong spring to propel the body into the air. Thrust powerfully against the floor with the entire surface of the sole of the foot. Bend the ankle, knee, and hip joints, and then stretch them as you leap.

3. When your body is in the air, tense the abdominal and hip muscles.

4. It is difficult to deliver an effective kick if you lean backward during the leap. Moreover, this lean contributes to an unbalanced landing position. A slight forward lean is recommended when applying a jump kick.

5. Absorb the landing shock with a flexible ankle and knee.

6. In the double jump kick, deliver the first attack with a short, sharp kick as you rise into the air. The second attack travels a greater distance, is more powerful, and hits the target at the peak of your leap. Apply both kicks with a strong snapping motion. Snap the second kick forward at the instant you begin to retract the first. In the jumping side kick fully lock out the knee of the kicking leg. Also, stiffen the ankle and foot of the kicking leg to strengthen the foot edge, and bring the opposite leg upward in front of the body. Jump as high as possible to facilitate a strong downward kick. It is unnecessary to jump a long distance.

Instructor H. Shirai (Italy) performs a
tobi-yoko-geri countering H. Ochi's kick.
Ochi was winner of the All-Japan Karate
Championships in 1966.

● *Training Method for Jumping Side Kick*

    1.   Assume the right-front stance with the hips relatively low.

    2.   Shift your weight to the right leg, thrust it hard against the ground, and spring upward.

    3.   As you rise into the air, raise the right leg and bring the heel up close to the inner thigh. Simultaneously, thrust the left leg outward and downward, to the side, kicking the target with the foot edge.

    4.   Withdraw the left leg, bring the right foot down toward the ground, and land. Keep the knee and ankle flexible to decrease the landing shock. Before practicing the jumping side kick, first rehearse the movement to be made by the right foot while you remain standing. Then sit on the floor and practice the position to be taken by both legs.

● *Training Method for Double Jump Kick I*

1.   Assume the informal attention stance.

2.   Support your weight with the right leg and raise the left leg with the knee close to the chest.

3.   Thrust against the ground with the right leg and leap upward. Continue to raise the right leg, bend the knee, and deliver a snap kick with the right foot.

4.   Land with the left leg, bring the right foot to the ground, and return to the position in #2.

5.   Return to the informal attention stance.

● *Training Method for Double Jump Kick II*

1.   Assume the right-front stance or the cat stance.

2.   Lower the hips slightly, thrust strongly against the ground with the right leg, and spring upward.

3.   As you rise into the air, raise and fully bend the left knee and deliver a strong, sharp snap kick with the left foot. Simultaneously, keep raising and bending the right knee and bring the right heel toward the buttocks.

4.   The instant the left foot begins its withdrawal from the target, snap the right foot forward with a large, strong movement.

5.   Return the right leg instantly to a position under the body and land with the left foot.

Instructor T. Okazaki (left) sidesteps Instructor H. Nishiyama's mae-geri and counters with a masterful example of tobi-yoko-geri.

● *Special Considerations*

1.   The legs often lack tension while the body is in the air. Keep the legs tightly drawn up under you before and after the kick hits the target. Prevent the legs from merely hanging loosely at any time during the leap.

2.   Do not consider the jump kick only from the height attained by the jump. Think of it as a jump that will allow you to deliver your kick effectively.

3.   Because the landing is the most dangerous part of this technique, judge your landing carefully and prepare for the next move. If you lose your balance in landing, the opponent can easily attack.

Basic Practice in Keri (kicking)

(Refer to the series of photos on pages 168 and 169.)

Yoko-geri (side kick)—A

1.   Assume the informal attention stance.

2.   Raise the left knee until the sole of the left foot touches the inside of the knee of the supporting leg.

3.   Deliver a side snap or a side thrust with the left leg.

4.   Return to the position in #2.

5.   Slowly return the left foot to the ground and resume the informal attention stance.

6.   Raise the right knee until the sole of the right foot touches the inside of the knee of the supporting leg.

7.   Deliver a side snap or a side thrust with the right leg.

8.   Return to the position in #6.

9.   Return to the informal attention stance.

Yoko-geri (side kick)—B

1.   Assume the straddle-leg stance.

2.   Shift your weight to the left leg. Move your right foot across the top of the left foot, and place it on the other side.

3.   Shift your weight to the right leg. Simultaneously, raise the left leg so that the foot passes behind the knee of the supporting leg.

4.   Deliver a snap kick or a thrust kick with the left leg.

5.   Return the left foot to the left side of the knee of the supporting leg and then slowly assume the straddle-leg stance.

6.   Shift your weight to the right leg. Move your left foot across the top of the right foot and place it on the other side.

7.   Shift your weight to the left leg. Simultaneously raise the right leg so that the foot passes behind the knee of the supporting leg.

8.   Deliver a snap kick or a thrust kick with the right leg.

9.   Return the right foot to the right side of the knee of the supporting leg and then slowly assume the straddle-leg stance.

Mawashi-geri (round kick)

1.   Assume the informal attention stance.

2.   Rotate your body clockwise until you face to your right, and raise your left leg to the side with the heel held close to the buttocks.

3.   Rotate the hips still further clockwise and deliver the round kick with a snap.

4.   Return to the position in #2 by rotating the hips counterclockwise.

5.   Return slowly to the informal attention stance.

6.   Practice the round kick on the opposite side of the body.

Side Kick   (B)

Round Kick

Side Kick   (A)

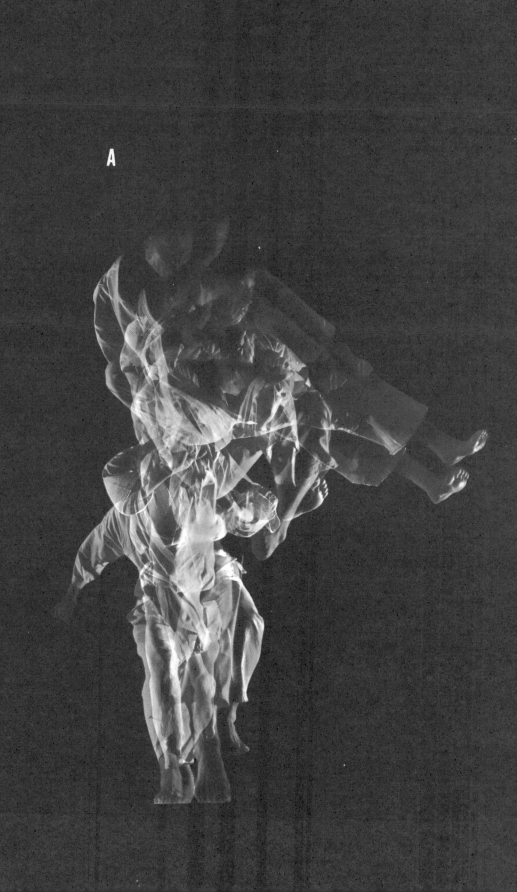

A

Because of the lightning-like speed of karate techniques, normal camera work often fails to record a punch of a kick adequately. The photographs on pages 170—173 were taken with the use of a stroboscope with the flashing capacity of 1/10,000 or a second. The photographs were taken from two different directions with two cameras.

Photograph A — Instructor H. Shirai performs *tobi-yoko-geri* (jumping side kick). Notice how the leap begins with a powerful spring, and how the kicking foot is thrust outward and slightly downward to the side at the peak of the leap.

Photograph B — Instructor T. Asai performs *nidan-geri* (double jump kick). The two kicks delivered during this cat-like jump possess devastating power. Observe how the legs and hips cushion the shock of landing.

B

C

Photograph C — Instructor Y. Yaguchi performs *yoko-kekomi* (side-thrust kick). The strong outward thrust of the fully bent kicking leg makes *soku-to* (foot edge) as sharp as a sword.

Photograph D — Instructor H. Kanazawa performs *tameshi-wari* (test of technique's power). He is breaking two boards, demonstrating the destructive power of a karate kick.

D

Chapter 8

Uke (Blocking) Theory and Practice

Characteristics of Blocking Techniques

Defense against an attack in karate is a more complicated process than it appears at first glance. To begin with, you must anticipate the nature and direction of your opponent's attack before blocking it. Also, while blocking, you must attempt to seize the initiative and turn the opponent's attack to your advantage.

The following methods illustrate the various possibilities in blocking.

1. Block the opponent's arm or leg with sufficient force to discourage further attack. In a sense, this kind of block can be called an attack.

2. Block the opponent's attack with only enough force to parry or deflect it. This would be termed a light block in #1.

3. Block and attack. Block the opponent's attack and immediately counter-attack. It is also possible to block and counterattack at the same instant.

4. Unbalance the opponent with your block.

5. Block the opponent's attack as it is about to begin. To do this you must anticipate his attack.

6. Block and then retreat to a safe position until a chance to counter presents itself.

Blocks against kicks are highly developed in karate. Kicks directed at vital areas of the body are usually absent in other body contact sports, and therefore

X-block

Side Two-hand Block

Hand Sweeping Block

Downward Block   **Hooking Knife-hand Block**

these blocking techniques are unique. In karate, not only the arms and hands are used to block kicks, but the feet and legs can be used as well.

As mentioned above, a strong block is a kind of attack because it can impart a strong shock to the opponent's arm or leg. The true and traditional meaning of karate is evident in this action. Stories are told of a karate master whose blocks were so powerful that his opponents felt as though his arms and legs were made of iron. Assailants attempting to attack him could not bear the pain of his blocks and were forced to retreat. To defend yourself without destroying others shows the true martial art spirit.

Many karate students today spend time in training for contests, concentrating on techniques that will win matches. They emphasize the use of combination techniques and stress the principle of continuous attack with a variety of techniques, rather than fundamental training in basic movements which will strengthen the arms, hands, and feet. It is helpful to study contest techniques, but training in the basic techniques peculiar to karate is much more important. The karate student seems to overlook the fact that a defense, if it is applied with sufficient force, can also be an attack. The ultimate aim of both offensive and defensive techniques is to prevent the opponent from continuing his attack. This point is worthy of consideration.

Basic Blocks

The following factors underlie karate blocking techniques.

Factor 1.   Direction of Power in the Block

First, correctly judge the path of the opponent's attack. Then, change the direction of his attack by blocking. Basically, blocks should be directed along these general routes:

A.   Against an attack to the face, block from the underneath upward.

B.   Against an attack to the midsection, block from the outside inward or vice versa.

C.   Against an attack against the groin area or lower, block downward and sweep to the side.

A block that lacks definite direction will usually fail. The principles set down above are evident in the following commonly used blocks.

● *Direction of Block in Jōdan-age-uke* (*upper block against head attack*)

1.   Move the blocking arm from its starting position upward and forward until it contacts the opponent's arm. At the moment of contact bring your forearm back toward your head, ending in a position directly in front of your forehead. In its complete course the blocking arm describes a curve. Note that its route lies outside the withdrawing arm. If you are greatly superior to your opponent in strength and skill, it is unnecessary to bring your forearm toward your head after blocking. Its path need not curve, but can continue upward and forward. However, under ordinary circumstances it is safer to follow the curve.

176

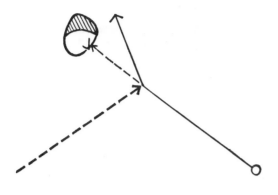

2. If your left hand is in front of your forehead as you begin your block, open the hand, point the fingers upward, and direct the edge of the hand outward. Withdraw the hand to a position above the left hip, dropping it straight down in front of the nose. Form a fist as it reaches the hip.

Move the right forearm upward as the left hand withdraws. The blocking arm's course is outside the left arm. If correctly done, the left hand and right forearm will form a cross in front of the face as they pass one another. Remember to keep the right elbow close to the body at the beginning of the block. The blocking surface in this defense includes about three or four inches of the bony area at the bottom of the wrist.

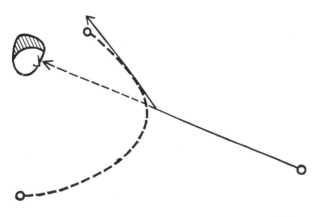

● *Direction of Block in Chūdan-ude-uke (forearm block against body attack)*

1. *Soto-uke (block from outside inward with bottom of wrist)*

Raise the left arm at the side with the fist near the left ear. At this point the bottom of the fist points outward toward the left. With the elbow bent at 90 degrees, drive the arm downward and forward and block the opponent's punch to your body. At the instant your forearm meets the opponent's arm the back of your fist must face the opponent at the height of your chin, with your forearm almost perpendicular to the ground. Twist the forearm 180 degrees counterclockwise as it travels from outside inward. To summarize, strike the opponent's attacking arm to the side with a circular motion of your forearm from the outside inward. As in the upper block technique, the blocking surface of the forearm is the bony area at the bottom of the wrist.

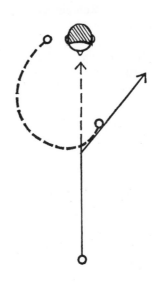

2. *Uchi-uke (block from inside outward with top of wrist)*

Place the left fist in front of the right hip with the back of the fist facing forward. Bring the forearm up and forward, using the elbow as a pivot. Deflect the opponent's body attack by striking his forearm to the side with the top of your wrist from the inside outward. The left hand travels forward outside the right. At the moment of contact be sure your elbow is bent at 90 degrees, your fist is at chin height, and your forearm is almost perpendicular to the ground.

Withdraw the right hand to a position above the right hip as your left forearm moves forward to block. Rotate the hips clockwise as you withdraw your right hand. Synchronize the hand and hip movements for additional power. The more power generated by the hip movement, the stronger will be your block.

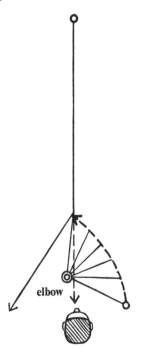

elbow

179

● *Direction of Block in Gedan-barai* (*downward block*)

Start the downward block with the left fist beside the right ear. Aim the back of the fist outward to the side. Strike downward, straightening the elbow, and deflect to the side the opponent's attack with the bottom of your wrist. End the downward block with the left fist directly above the left knee.

● *Direction of Block in Chūdan-shutō-uke* (*knife-hand block against body attack*)

Place the right knife-hand beside the left ear with the back of the hand facing outward to the side. Snap the right hand forward and rotate the body counterclockwise. As the hand moves forward to block, rotate the forearm counterclockwise and keep the elbow bent.

Concentrate on mastering the blocks designed to parry the various attacks. Remember that your block will be stronger if it travels a longer route to its destination. Although this longer route is desirable, it is usually not possible because there is only limited time in which to block. Because they must respond to attacks of great speed and suddenness, advanced students inevitably do not begin their blocks from the positions outlined above. However, beginners must master the block in its full and correct course before they can expect to use a shortened version of it. In every case, beginners must concentrate on learning basic techniques.

Direction of Downward Block. Draw a large arc with the elbow as the axis

Direction of Knife-hand Block. Draw a smaller arc with the elbow as the axis

Factor 2. Forearm Rotation and Timing

Forearm Rotation

Blocks gain in power if you rotate the forearm during the delivery. When you block, twist your forearm as though you intended to drive it into the bone of the opponent's arm. This forearm rotation also serves to guide the opponent's attack away from your body.

● *Jōdan-age-uke* (*rising block against head attack*)

Rotate the forearm counterclockwise as you raise it to your forehead. Keep the elbow bent throughout. Tense the wrist and the forearm muscles.

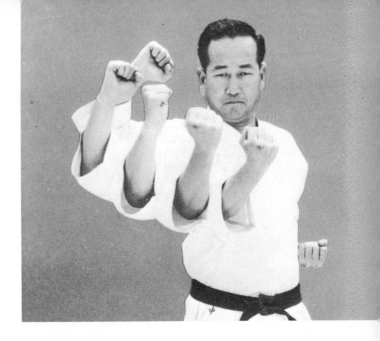

● *Chūdan-ude-uke* (*forearm block against body attack*)
Soto-uke (block from outside inward): Rotate the forearm clockwise as you block. Keep the elbow bent throughout.
● *Uchi-uke* (block from inside outward): Rotate the forearm clockwise as you bring it forward to block.

● *Shutō-uke* (*knife-hand block*)
From the inside outward: Rotate the forearm counterclockwise as you block. Keep your elbow bent throughout.
From the outside inward: Rotate the forearm clockwise.

● *Gedan-barai* (*downward block*)
Rotate the forearm inward, straighten the elbow, and block with a big downward motion of the arm.

● *Timing*

Forearm rotation and timing are closely related. Obviously, the block must not be applied too early or too late. Judge the opponent's intent and assume the starting position of your block, but be sure to allow enough time to parry or deflect the attack.

Let us consider the upper block, under ideal conditions, in terms of forearm rotation and timing. As explained above, raise and rotate your forearm from the side, and block the opponent's arm upward from below. Contact the attacking arm relatively far from your head before bringing your arm back toward your head. After the initial contact, continue to rotate your forearm to guide the opponent's attack up over your head.

Sometimes the opponent is too close to enable you to block his arm in the manner outlined above. In such a situation quickly raise your forearm straight upward, rotating it rapidly. Because the opportunity to guide the attacking arm away from you is absent, the block must be strong and sharp enough to deflect the attack. Correct timing and arm rotation are essential if the block is to be effective.

Unfortunately, ideal blocking conditions are seldom met. There is usually insufficient time to assume the prescribed starting position. When the attack comes suddenly, move immediately into the final phase of the block from whatever position you may be in.

In the case of an attack directed at your abdomen, you may be confronted with a choice of blocks. Hesitation could prove disastrous, as could the wrong choice. To illustrate, suppose you are in a low position and the opponent attacks your solar plexus, or suppose a taller opponent attacks this point. You are faced with a choice of blocks. If you block with the downward block, first raising your fist to your shoulder, you will have insufficient time for a successful block because your fist will be raised too high. Far better would be the forearm block against a body attack from the outside inward. Attain proficiency in the appropriate block through constant practice.

To have sufficient time and space to enable the blocking arm to achieve somewhere near its full range of movement is not always possible. However, because blocking conditions are usually less than ideal, correct timing becomes extremely important. Gauge the speed of the opponent's attack and his distance from you, and then time your block to deflect his attack.

Factor 3.   Hip Rotation

The discussion of punching techniques clearly demonstrated the importance of hip rotation to increase punching power. Hip rotation is also necessary to produce an effective block. Whether your block is to be a strong one, delivered from a solidly based position, or a light one, delivered from a moving and flexible position, remember to rotate your hips. It is impossible to parry or deflect a strong attack if you fail to use the power in the hips.

In blocking, both arms appear to start moving at the same time. However, a closer analysis of the movement reveals that the blocking arm lags an instant behind the withdrawing arm at the start. In the upper block, the left hand begins the movement, then the left arm, the shoulders, and the hips move. As part of this movement the right arm moves upward to block. In other words, the withdrawing arm moves first. The order of movement in the block from the outside inward against a body attack is similar to that in the upper block except for the difference in arm positions and in blocking direction.

If the hips have been properly rotated in the block, an automatic hip reversal takes place which aids greatly in applying a counter. Put another way, when the hips have rotated fully in one direction, and the limit of tension is reached in the abdominal region, the hips will begin to rotate in the opposite direction. Power from this counter-rotation flows toward and is increased by the shoulders, upper arm, and forearm, and ends in the fist as a powerful explosion against the target.

Despite the fact that in the upper block and in the forearm block against a body attack the withdrawing arm moves a split second before the blocking arm, the following components of the movement all end at the same instant:

1.   the withdrawal of the fist of the non-blocking arm to a position above the hip;

2.   the assumption of *hanmi*; and

3.   the application of the block.

Instructor K. Enoeda (face showing) and Instructor H. Shirai face each other in a silent duel.

Photos illustrate priority in course of blocking movement. Movement begins with withdrawing arm, shifts instantly to hips, and then to blocking arm.

Upper Block against head attack

Forearm Block against body attack

Block will fail if elbow is not close enough to body. Armpit and side muscles cannot be tensed

B

A

Knife-hand Block against body correctly executed

  C

Factor 4. Position of Elbow of Blocking Arm

The instant the block is applied, all power must be concentrated in the forearm. The amount of power you are able to exert depends on the relationship of your elbow to the side of your body. If your elbow is too far removed from your body, it will be difficult to tense the muscles at your side, and your block will be weak. Also, if your elbow remains too close to your body when you block, the scale of your block will be small, and the blocking power reduced. Keep your elbow neither too far away nor too close to your body. Moreover, when blocking body attacks, ensure that your forearm ends its movement in the center of your body rather than to the left or right. If your elbow and forearm are correctly positioned, the power of hips, body, and arm will be concentrated in the forearm. At the moment of impact, fully tense your side and arm muscles.

A discussion of correct elbow position in the various blocks follows.

● *Age-uke* (*upper block*)

Raise your elbow to the height of your ear and as close as possible to it. This location enables your body to provide adequate tension.

● *Chūdan-ude-uke* (*forearm block against body attack*)

Place your elbow a palm's width away from your side when you stand in *hanmi*. If more than double this distance separates the elbow from the side, it will be difficult to tense the muscles at the side. Position your elbow so it roughly bisects your body when you stand in *hanmi*. A punch from directly ahead should either hit your forearm or be deflected harmlessly to either side of your body.

Avoid moving your elbow in any direction away from the prescribed position. Your block will fail if your elbow leaves your side to the front as illustrated in photo A on page 188. Photograph B also shows the elbow too far removed to one side of the prescribed position.

● *Chūdan-shutō-uke* (*knife-hand block against body attack*)

The elbow position corresponds to that suggested for the forearm block. In photo C the elbow is too far removed to one side of the ideal position.

Upper Block correctly done

Upper Block; elbow raised too high.

Factor 5. Terminal Position of Block

It serves no useful purpose to swing the forearm past the point where the block was effected. If your forearm continues its movement after blocking, tension of the side muscles will be lost, control of the body reduced, and the follow-up technique difficult to apply. If you swing your forearm beyond the recommended position without stopping to focus the block, it is likely that your block will fail. Under such circumstances a prime requirement for a strong block—tension of the side muscles—cannot be met. Recommended terminal positions for the various blocks follow.

● *Jōdan-age-uke* (*upper block against head attack*)

End the block with your forearm the distance of one fist in front of your forehead. In this position your forearm should be at an angle to the horizontal. (See photo at left, above.) If you block in this way, the opponent's attack will pass over your head. Also, the time spent in blocking is kept to a minimum, compared with a block which does not stop in front of the forehead but continues further upward.

Photo D illustrates an incorrect position of the blocking arm. The elbow is raised excessively, and balance is impaired. Shifting to the following technique will prove difficult.

● *Chūdan-ude-uke* (*forearm block against body attack*)

Photo E shows an example of excessive blocking. A straight line drawn from the inside of the blocking forearm to the left side of the body does not correspond to the direction of the opponent's attack. Although the body is not unbalanced, the forearm has traveled past the point recommended for a correct block.

● *Chūdan-shutō-uke* (*knife-hand block against body attack*)

A straight line drawn from the edge of the hand to the shoulder of the blocking arm must correspond to the direction of the opponent's attack. Photos F and G both illustrate incorrect blocking positions. In F the blocking arm is too straight. and in G it is too close to the body.

Knife-hand Block correctly done

Forearm Block correctly done

Knife-hand Block arm excessively extended

F

Forearm Block against body attack

Knife-hand Block; arm insufficiently extended, technique too small

G

Forearm Block; fist swung further than necessary

E

Factor 6. Blocks as Attacks

As mentioned, a block can also serve as an attack. For example, a powerful block can deliver a shock strong enough to discourage further attack. There is another sense, however, in which blocking movements can serve as attacks. For instance, as the forearm blocks, the hand of the blocking arm can simultaneously strike the opponent's nose or chin. This characteristic of karate is absent from other martial arts. A study of the various blocks reveals many interesting uses.

● *Age-uke* (*upper block*)

The upper block can be used as an attack in the following way. When the opponent attacks your head with a punch, lower your hips, lean slightly forward and step in under the attacking arm. At the same time apply the upper block in such a way that you simultaneously attack his armpit with your elbow and his chin with the bottom of your fist. (See photo on page 188.)

Another possibility for the upper block as an attack occurs immediately after blocking. With the hand of your blocking arm, grasp the wrist of the opponent's attacking arm and pull downward, simultaneously applying the upper block with your other arm to his elbow joint.

● *Ude-uke* (*forearm block*) *and Shutō-uke* (*knife-hand block*)

As your opponent moves forward to attack your body with a punch, step into his attack and block with a wide-sweeping forearm or knife-hand block. Your purpose is to block his attack and at the same time to strike the point under his nose with your fist, or to poke his eyes with your fingers. (See photos on pages 194 and 195.)

● *Hiji-suri-uke* (*elbow sliding block*)

This is a combination block and punch. As the opponent attacks your face with a right lunge punch, step back with your right foot and thrust your left arm upward in an upper block. However, do not complete the upper block. Instead, flip the attacking arm slightly to the side with your elbow and then thrust your fist forward to the opponent's face. (See photos on pages 194–95.)

**Fumikomi-age-uke
(upper block, stepping in)**

**Fumikomi-ude-uke
(forearm block, stepping in)**

**Fumikomi-shutō-uke
(knife-hand block, stepping in)**

**Hiji-suri-uke
(elbow sliding block)**

**Hiji-suri-uke
(elbow sliding block)**

Training method   (1)

Basic Blocking Techniques and Training Methods
● *Jōdan-age-uke* (*upper block against head attack*)
The upper block is one of the basic techniques used to block attacks aimed higher than the solar plexus. When the opponent attempts to attack your face with a punch, block his attack with the bottom of your wrist by raising your arm powerfully upward.
● *Important Points*
1.   Complete your block with your forearm about four inches in front of your forehead, the hand higher than the elbow, and the bottom of your fist facing up. Avoid allowing your elbow to deviate from the most direct route to its terminal position. It should move forward and upward close to the side of the body.
2.   Keep a 90 degree angle in the elbow of your blocking arm as you raise it. Withdraw the opposite arm to a position above the hip. The arms should cross one another at chin height. Rotate the forearms as they move in opposite directions. Be sure to execute the arm movements crisply and powerfully.
3.   The moment you block the opponent's attack, tighten your fist. Simultaneously, strongly tense your abdominal muscles and transmit this tension to the muscles around your armpit and to the blocking arm in a wave-like flow of power.

196

● *Training Method for Jōdan-age-uke: 1*

1.   Assume the left-front stance, with hips and shoulders squarely forward.

2.   Place your right forearm in front of your forehead with the hand open, palm facing outward. Position your left fist above the left hip with the back of the fist directed downward.

3.   Rotate your hips clockwise and begin to pull your right hand down in front of your nose toward your right hip.   At the same time, raise your left forearm, rotating it as it rises. The course of the left arm lies to the outside of the right.

4.   As you withdraw your right hand toward your side, form a fist. Raise your left forearm to the height of your forehead. Complete the blocking movement at the same instant your body finishes its shift to *hanmi*.

5.   Rotate your hips counterclockwise and return to the position described in #2. Return your hands also to the initial position.

6.   Repeat the above practice on both sides of the body. After you become accustomed to Training Method 1, begin the practice outlined in Training Method 2.

● *Training Method for Jōdan-age-uke: 2*

1. Assume the open-leg stance at *Shizen-tai*.

2. Begin to slide your right foot to the rear and raise your right arm in front of your face. As your foot continues to the rear, withdraw the right hand to your right side and bring your left forearm upward to block. Raise the blocking arm to the outside of the withdrawing arm.

3. At the end of the blocking movement your body should be at *hanmi*, your right fist above your right hip, and your left forearm in front of your forehead. (See illustration.)

4. Return to your initial position.

5. Practice the above movement alternately on both sides of the body.

● *Important Considerations*

1. If you raise the elbow of your blocking arm too high, the muscles around your armpit cannot tense fully and your block will be weak. (See photo on page 199.) Avoid this fault by blocking with your hand higher than your elbow.

2. If your blocking forearm ends too far in advance of your forehead, the opponent's attack may pass over your block and hit you. (See photo 1, page 213.) Remember that the ideal distance separating your forehead and forearm is four inches.

3. Sometimes fear of the impending attack causes students to throw their heads backward to escape the blow. Avoid this reaction.

● *Age-uke* (*gyaku-ashi*) (*upper block* [*reverse foot*]) In this blocking technique, block with your right arm while standing in the left-front stance, or with your left arm while standing in the right-front stance. If you block with your right arm, step to the rear with your right foot and rotate your hips counterclockwise.

If blocking forearm is too far from forehead, opponent's attack will connect

If elbow of blocking arm is too high, block will be ineffective

199

Training method   (1)

Training method   (2)

● *Chūdan-ude-uke* (*soto-uke*) (*forearm block against body attack* [*from outside inward*])

This technique provides an excellent means of blocking the opponent's punch to your body. In this block, deflect the opponent's arm to the side as you block from the outside inward. If applied with sufficient force, this block alone is powerful enough to discourage further attack.

● *Important Points*

1. In the terminal position of the block, be sure your arm is bent 90 degrees at the elbow and that your forearm is almost perpendicular to the ground. At this point your elbow should be about four inches from your side, and the upper margin of your fist at chin height. Fully tense the muscles around your armpit.

During the forward movement of the blocking arm, withdraw the opposite arm to your side, tightly forming a fist as though you meant to grasp something. Rotate your hips as part of the block. The power generated by hip rotation will be transmitted to your blocking arm.

● *Training Method for Chūdan-ude-uke* (*soto-uke*): *1*

1. Assume the right-front stance, with hips and shoulders squarely forward.

2. Stretch the left hand out in front at solar plexus height. The hand may be open or in a fist, but in either case the back of the hand faces up. Place your right hand over your right shoulder next to your ear.

3. Withdraw your left hand to your left side, revolving it 180 degrees counterclockwise. If your hand is open, form a fist as it approaches the hip. Rotate your hips counterclockwise. At the same time, drive your right arm forward from the outside inward, and block. Rotate your blocking forearm clockwise as you swing it forward.

4. End the block with your body at *hanmi*, your left fist over your left hip (back of fist facing down), and the upper margin of your right fist at chin height.

5. Return to the position described in #2.

6. Repeat the above practice on both sides of your body.

● *Training Method for Chūdan-ude-uke (soto-uke): 2*

1.   Assume the open-leg stance of the natural position. Let your arms hang naturally at the sides.

2.   Begin a backward step with your left foot and extend your left hand (or fist) to the front. Simultaneously, raise your right fist above your right shoulder near the ear.

3.   Continue your backward step, withdraw the left hand to the left side, and rotate the hips counterclockwise. At the same time, drive the right forearm forward from the outside inward against the imaginary attacking arm.

4.   End the entire blocking movement with your body in the right-front stance at *hanmi*. At this moment your left fist belongs over your left hip with the back of the fist directed down, and your right fist belongs in front of your body with its upper margin at chin height.

5.   Step forward with the left foot and return to the position described in #1.

6.   Practice this blocking technique on the other side of your body by blocking with your left arm. Finally, repeat the movement alternately on both sides.

Instead of stepping to the rear when blocking, practice also while stepping forward. In addition, necessary training includes applying the block after shifting to the back stance and the straddle-leg stance.

→

● *Special Considerations*

1. Rotate your hips strongly. The faster the hips rotate, the greater the strength they impart to the block. Increase the speed of your hip rotation by powerfully withdrawing your non-blocking arm. Avoid rotating only your shoulders when it is necessary to rotate your hips.

2. Blocking failure is more likely if you block the opponent's attack diagonally from above downward. Block in such a way that the attack is deflected to the side. In the terminal position of the block, avoid allowing the elbow of your blocking arm to deviate in any direction from the recommended position.

3. Bend the blocking arm 90 degrees at the elbow. Avoid straightening or bending your elbow excessively.

4. Your block will be ineffective if the wrist of your blocking arm is bent. Straighten and firmly tighten it.

● *Chūdan-ude-uke* (*uchi-uke*) (*forearm block against body attack* [*from inside outward*])

Use this technique to block the opponent's body attack by sweeping your forearm from the inside outward and deflecting his attack to the side.

● *Important Points*

1. The main points made regarding the outside inward block apply also to the inside outward. The important difference between them lies in the direction of the blocking movement.

2. Withdraw the non-blocking arm and rotate your hips. At the same time, drive the blocking forearm from the inside outward. The blocking arm's course lies to the outside of the withdrawing arm.

● *Training Method for Chūdan-ude-uke* (*uchi-uke*): *1*

1. Assume the left-front stance with the shoulders and hips squarely forward.

2. Extend your right hand forward, palm down, and place your left fist in front of your right hip, with the back of the fist facing up.

3. Withdraw your right hand toward your right hip and rotate your hips clockwise. At the same time, drive your left forearm forward on a course to the outside of the withdrawing arm. Use your elbow as a pivot as you rotate the blocking forearm counterclockwise, and block from the inside outward.

4. End the block with your body in *hanmi*. At this point, your right fist should be above your right hip, and your left forearm almost perpendicular to the ground, with the upper margin of the fist at chin height.

5. Rotate your hips counterclockwise and return to the position described in #2.

6. Practice this technique alternately on both sides of the body.

Training method   (1)

Training method   (2)

● *Training Method for Chūdan-ude-uke* (*uchi-uke*)*:2*
1.   Assume the open-leg stance of the natural position.
2.   Begin a step backward with your left foot. Simultaneously extend your left hand forward, palm down, and place your right fist in front of your left hip with the back of the fist facing up.
3.   As your foot continues backward, withdraw your left hand to your left side and rotate your hips counterclockwise. At the same time, swing your right arm forward from the inside outward. Use your elbow as a pivot and rotate your forearm clockwise as you swing it forward.
4.   End your block with your body in the right-front stance at *hanmi*. The block might just as easily have ended in the straddle-leg stance or the back stance. Whatever the terminal position, the left fist must end above the left hip with the back of the fist facing down.
5.   Step forward and return to the position described in #1.
6.   Repeat the above practice alternately on both sides of the body.
Instead of stepping back to render this blocking technique, practice it by stepping forward into the front stance, the straddle-leg stance, or the back stance.
● *Special Considerations*
1.   The inside outward block will be weak if you block with the arm alone. Use the power generated by hip rotation to strengthen your block.
2.   Avoid blocking with only one arm. Use both arms. In other words, this technique will not exert maximum power unless the non-blocking arm is swiftly and strongly withdrawn.
3.   The position of the elbow of the blocking arm should change very little during the entire blocking movement. Drive the forearm outward as if it were a fan opening. The elbow acts as the pivot of this circular forearm motion.
Soto-uke and *uchi-uke* are usually practiced as blocks against body attacks, but they are also effective against attacks to the head.

● *Otoshi-uke* (*dropping block*)

Use this technique to block an attack against your abdomen. Drop your forearm straight down from above your head and block the opponent's forearm with the bottom of your wrist. The terminal position of the block should see your forearm parallel to the ground, with the back of the fist facing forward.

The dropping block is similar to the forearm block against a body attack, but differs from the latter in the route it takes to the target. Note also that the opponent's arm is driven downward rather than to the side as in the forearm block.

● *Gedan-barai or Gedan-uke* (*downward block*)

Block the opponent's punch or kick to your lower abdomen with the downward block. Deflect his attack to the side by driving your forearm downward and slightly sideward. This is one of the basic blocks against an attack to the lower part of your body.

● *Important Points*

1. End the downward block with the fist of the blocking arm about six inches above the knee of the forward leg.

2. Direct the blocking and withdrawing forearms in such a way that the two almost touch as they move in their respective directions. Rotate both forearms during the course of the block.

3. Because you may be required to block a powerful kick, your block must be correspondingly strong. Block with a big downward motion of the blocking arm.

● *Training Method for Gedan-barai*

1. Assume the left-front stance, with shoulders and hips squarely forward.

2. Extend your right arm in front of your abdomen with the back of the hand facing up. The hand can either remain open or form a fist. Raise your left fist to a position just beside your right ear, with the back of the fist facing outward to the side.

3. Withdraw your right hand to your right side and rotate your hips clockwise. At the same time, drive your left forearm downward. Rotate the forearm clockwise and straighten the elbow as your blocking arm descends.

4. End block with your body in the left-front stance at *hanmi*. The fist of your left (blocking) arm should be about six inches above your left knee with the back of the fist facing up.

5. Return to the position described in #2.

6. Repeat the above practice alternately on both sides of the body.

● *Training Method for Gedan-barai*

1.   Assume the open-leg stance of the natural position.

2.   Begin a backward step with your right foot, extend your right arm in front of your lower abdomen and place your left fist beside your right ear.

3.   Continue stepping backward, withdraw your right hand to your side, forming a fist, and rotate your hips clockwise. Simultaneously, drive your left forearm downward, rotating the forearm and straightening the elbow.

4.   End the downward block with your body in the left-front stance at *hanmi*. Your right fist should be above your right hip with its back facing down. Your left arm should end above your forward leg with the back of the fist facing up.

5.   Advance the rear foot one step and return to the position in #1.

6.   Practice this technique on the opposite side of the body.

Repeat the above training alternately on both sides of the body.

Additional practice consists of applying the downward block while stepping forward instead of to the rear and also from other stances.

● *Special Considerations*

1.   If you are afraid of the opponent's attack, you are apt to withdraw your hips to avoid being hit. This action weakens the downward block. It is difficult to block a powerful kick if your body leans forward. Push your hips forward during the block to maintain your body perpendicular to the ground.

2.   If you attempt a downward block without fully rotating your hips, your block may prove ineffective. Because the opponent's kick to your groin is very powerful, place special emphasis on hip rotation to generate the strength necessary.

3.   If your hips are too high as you block, the opponent's chances of delivering a successful attack increase. Keep your hips low and block from a position as close as possible to the opponent.

4.   If the fist of your blocking arm deviates from the recommended six inches above the forward knee, your block may fail. If your block ends too far above your knee, the opponent's kick will hit your abdomen. If it ends too close to your knee, your block will miss the kick completely and your chin will suffer the consequences. (See photos on page 207).

Block will fail if blocking arm is too high or too low.

● *Chūdan-shutō-uke*
(*knife-hand block against body attack*)
The knife-hand block is one of the fundamental blocks against an attack directed at the abdomen. Block the attack as though the edge of your hand were sharp and you intended to cut the opponent's hand off at the wrist. This technique is peculiar to karate, and is rather difficult to execute correctly. It has many variations.
● *Important Points*
   1.   The hand of the non-blocking arm is not withdrawn to the side, but stops in front of the solar plexus with the palm open, facing up. Use this hand to counter-

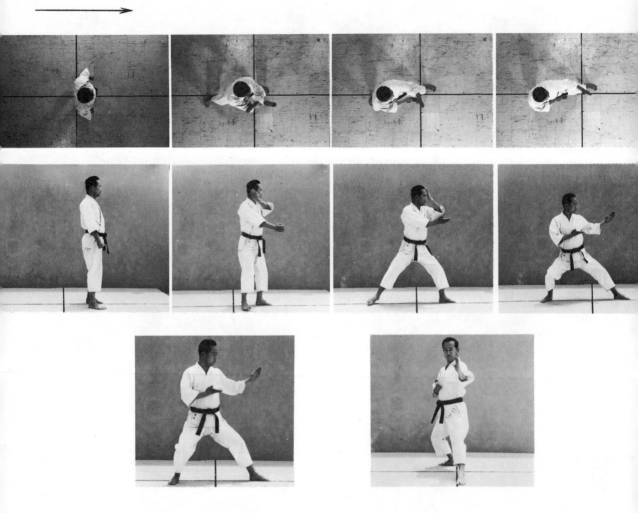

attack with *nukite* (spear-hand) immediately after applying the knife-hand block with the other hand.

2. At the terminal point of this block, be sure the elbow of the blocking arm is bent at 90 degrees, and that the muscles around the armpit are flexed. The elbow should not end its movement at one side of the body. Force the elbow inward.

3. The blocking hand travels a route diagonally forward and downward to the target from its starting position. This route lies above that of the withdrawing arm.

4. Withdraw your body diagonally to the rear. If you step "straight" backward, or block without stepping backward, this technique has little chance of success.

● *Training Method for Chūdan-shutō-uke*

1. Assume the open-leg stance of the natural position.

2. Begin a step to the rear with your right foot and extend your right hand to the front at solar plexus height, palm down. At the same time, place your left hand in knife-hand beside your right ear with the back of the hand facing outward to the side. Your left elbow should be just in front of the upper left side of your chest.

3. Continue to step to the rear. Your backward course may be diagonal or straight. Withdraw your right hand toward its position in front of the solar plexus, and rotate your hips clockwise. At the same time, drive your left hand forward and downward toward the target with a clockwise rotation of the forearm.

4. End the block in the right-back stance at *hanmi*, right hand in front of your solar plexus, palm facing up, and left arm in the correct blocking position.

5. Return your right foot to its initial place and return to the position in #1.

6. Practice the above movement on the opposite side of the body.

Knife-hand Block is very effective against head attack.

● *Special Considerations*

1. The two most commonly observed faults in the knife-hand block are (1) failure to bend the elbow of the blocking arm the required 90 degrees, and (2) failure to keep the wrist of the blocking arm straight. In the first instance, your hand will probably hit the bottom of the attacking arm, and in the second it will hit the top. Be sure to bend the elbow correctly and to keep the wrist straight.

2. In the terminal position of the block, the elbow of the blocking arm sometimes ends to the outside of the prescribed position. For example, when blocking with the left hand, the elbow may end at a point too far to the left of the body. This condition reduces blocking power. Tighten the muscles around the armpit and force the elbow toward the opposite side.

3. During the course of the block, the shoulder muscles tend to be flexed and the shoulder raised. This situation prevents flexing of the muscles around the armpit and side, producing an ineffective block. Relax the shoulder muscles to allow the shoulder to hang naturally throughout the block.

● *Tate-shutō* (*vertical knife-hand block*)
● *Kake-shutō-uke* (*hooking knife-hand block*)
These two blocks are almost the same. Bend the wrist of the blocking arm until the palm of the hand faces forward and the fingers point straight up. These blocks are useful against a punch directed at your solar plexus. Swing your forearm from the inside outward and deflect the attack to the side.

● *Important Points*

1. Contrary to the usual knife-hand block, block with the elbow of your blocking arm straight.

2. Maintain the wrist firm and strong in its bent position. Your block must be powerful or it will fail to deflect the attack.

3. Begin the vertical knife-hand block with the hand of the blocking arm near the ear of the opposite side. Swing the hand forward, straighten the elbow, and block the opponent's forearm from the inside outward.

This blocking technique is also effective against an attack from the side. To effect the block, swing your hand in a wide arc from the side of your body opposite the attack. End up with your arm stretched straight out to the side from your shoulder.

An opportunity often exists with the knife-hand block to grasp the opponent's arm or sleeve after blocking his attacking arm. Grasp his arm and pull him off balance as you counter his attack.

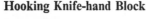

Hooking Knife-hand Block

● *Haishu-uke* (*back-hand block*)

The back-hand block is applied using the back of the hand. Direct the blocking hand against the opponent's upper arm, elbow, or forearm when he attempts to attack your solar plexus with a punch. Block with a snapping motion of your forearm.

● *Important Points*

1. Turn the side of your body toward the attack and strike the attacking arm with a snap of the forearm as in a back-fist strike. The block will be more effective if the position of your elbow remains fixed as you strike the opponent's arm.

2. Keep the line formed by the hand and wrist straight, and tighten the wrist. When using the back hand to block, tense the entire surface of the back of the hand.

Ox-jaw Block

Bent-Wrist Block   **Chicken-head Wrist Block**

Palm-heel Block

Blocks Performed with Special Areas of the Hand

Blocks are sometimes applied with special sections of the hand and wrist. Although the primary purpose of these blocks is to deflect the opponent's attack, they can be applied powerfully enough to impart a decisive shock.

● *Kakutō-uke* (*bent-wrist block*)

Bend your hand fully downward and inward toward the wrist. Block with that area of the wrist above the back of the hand given prominence by the bend. (See page 213 for position.) In the bent-wrist block, strike the opponent's attacking forearm from underneath upward with a powerful snap. This technique can also be used to deflect the attacking arm to the side by striking the arm from the side.

● *Keitō-uke* (*chicken-head wrist block*)

With the back of the hand facing outward to the side, fully depress the hand and use the base and first joint of the thumb to block. (See page 213 for position.) Strike the attacking forearm from underneath upward.

● *Seiryūtō-uke* (*ox-jaw block*)

With the back of the hand facing outward to the side, fully elevate the hand without moving the wrist. With the rounded section of the hand and wrist thus formed, block the opponent's forearm or leg. (See page 213 for position.) The ox-jaw block is used as a downward block.

● *Teishō-uke* (*palm-heel block*)

With the back of the hand facing up, fully elevate the hand and use the heel of the hand to block the opponent's forearm or leg. (See page 213 for position.) The palm-heel block can serve as an effective block in all directions—from underneath upward, from above downward, and from side to side.

● *Important Points*

1. The success of the above blocking techniques depends upon a strong wrist and forearm snap. Free the elbow of tension for maximum snap.

2. A strong block against the opponent's wrist, elbow joint, or shin with the above techniques will often discourage further attack.

→ **Use of Ox-jaw Block**

→ **Use of Palm-heel Block**

Bent-wrist Block

Chicken-head Wrist Block

Palm-heel Block

Ox-jaw Block

Back-Arm Sweeping Block

Hand Sweeping Block

Hand Pressing Block

Wrist-hook Block

● *Haiwan-nagashi-uke* (*back-arm sweeping block*)

Use this technique to block an opponent's punch directed at your face. If you choose to block with your right arm, begin by raising your right forearm in front of your body while simultaneously withdrawing your right hip and leg. Strike the opponent's arm upward with the bottom of your forearm and, without interrupting your movement, bring your forearm to the right side of your head.

● *Important Points*

1. As you assume the *hanmi* position, strike the opponent's attacking forearm upward. Continue to move your blocking forearm but change its direction by withdrawing it to a point beside your head to guide his attack past your head.

2. When withdrawing your forearm, direct its bottom surface outward to the side. The withdrawal route should resemble the shape of a crescent.

3. Ensure that the block ends with your elbow pointed straight to the side, your fist slightly above your ear, and the muscles around your armpit tensed.

● *Te-nagashi-uke* (*hand sweeping block*)

This block is used to parry an opponent's punch to your face. Extend your open hand in front of your body, palm facing outward. After contacting the opponent's forearm, withdraw your hand to guide his attack past your head.

● *Important Points*

1. Step backward with your right leg to assume *hanmi*, extend your left arm forward and bend your wrist until the fingers point straight upward. As soon as your left hand contacts the opponent's attacking arm, withdraw it to your right ear.

3. It is unnecessary to exert full power in the block. Concentrate instead on smoothly changing the course of the opponent's attack.

● *Te-osae-uke* (*hand pressing block*)

Employ this block when the opponent attempts a punch to your chest or solar plexus. As the opponent's punch moves toward you, contact his forearm with your hand from above, press downward, and draw his arm toward you.

● *Important Points*

1. Step backward with your right leg into the *hanmi* position as your left hand presses the top of the opponent's attacking forearm and restricts its advance.

2. As your hand applies pressure to the top of the opponent's forearm, bend the elbow of your blocking arm and ensure that your forearm is parallel to the ground. In this position draw the opponent's arm along its line of advance.

● *Tekubi-kake-uke* (*wrist-hook block*)

Use this block against a punch to your chest or solar plexus. Sidestep the opponent's punch and simultaneously block it, using your open hand and wrist like a reverse hook. Form the hook by bending your hand upward at the wrist.

● *Important Points*

1. From a position in front of your body, rotate your hand in a 270-degree arc upward and to the outside to hook the opponent's wrist downward from above. Think of your elbow as a fixed pivot around which your hand and forearm rotate.

2. Bend your blocking hand fully upward at the wrist and maintain this tension during the block. Also, tense the muscles around your armpit to prevent any variation in the position of your elbow.

3. As you block with your right arm, slide your right foot diagonally forward until your body is in *hanmi* slightly at one side of the opponent. The block, combined with this shift in position, should prove very effective.

● *Maeude-hineri-uke* (*forearm twist block*)

This block is effective against a punch directed at your face or chest. Rotate your hips clockwise and assume *hanmi*. Simultaneously, extend your right fist toward your opponent, contact the bottom of his wrist with your forearm, and then withdraw your forearm to your right side with a snapping counterclockwise rotation.

● *Important Points*

1. Time your block to the opponent's attack. As soon as you contact his arm, withdraw your forearm and rotate it to flip his attack aside.

2. Withdraw your blocking forearm until it is perpendicular to the ground. At the terminal position of the block the back of your hand must face forward and that portion of your wrist below your thumb must act as the blocking surface.

● *Maeude-deai-osae-uke* (*forearm pressing block*)

As the opponent begins his attack, bend your left elbow at 90 degrees, step forward with your left foot, and drive your left forearm into his arm.

● *Important Points*

1. Correct timing is essential to the success of this technique. You must anticipate the start of the attack, step forward, and block.

2. Avoid describing a curve with your blocking forearm. Instead, thrust your hips forward and drive your forearm directly to the target.

3. Merely pressing the opponent's forearm is ineffective. Drive your forearm into the crook of his elbow with maximum power.

Instructor K. Enoeda (right) blocks Instructor A. Takahashi's oi-zuki with a back-fist strike and counters further with a sokutō-kekomi.

Two-Handed Blocks

A very powerful punch or kick can be blocked by using a two-handed blocking technique. Descriptions of some two-handed blocks follow.

● *Morote-uke* (*augmented forearm block*)

1. When the opponent's attack is too powerful to block with the ordinary block from the inside outward with the top of the wrist, strengthen your block by bracing the blocking forearm with your other fist.

2. Be sure your bracing fist or open hand is in close contact with your blocking forearm just below the elbow. After blocking with the augmented forearm block you can easily counterattack with a back-fist strike.

3. This block is usually done by retreating as the opponent attacks. However, if you block while stepping into the attack, you can generate additional power.

● *Jūji-uke* (*X-block*)

To perform this technique, cross your hands at the wrist to form a kind of X. Using the forearms in this way makes a very powerful blocking technique possible.

● *Important Points*

1. If the opponent directs a punch at your face, you can easily deflect his attack by driving your crossed wrists upward into his forearm.

2. The X-block can be done with open hands as well as with fists.

Front kicks can also be effectively blocked with this technique. Block the attacking leg either at the ankle or just above the knee by powerfully driving your crossed wrists toward the target. As you block be sure to thrust your hips forward and to keep your body perpendicular to the ground. If you withdraw your hips, as in the photo on page 219, your block will be weak and the opponent's kick may reach its target.

● *Sokumen-awase-uke* (*side combined block*)

When an opponent standing at your side directs a punch at the side of your head, use this block to deflect his attack. Bend both hands upward at the wrists, arrange the hands so that the backs touch, and the fingers point upward. Deflect the attack with the palm of one hand reinforced by the back of the other hand.

Augmented Forearm Block

Side Combined Block

X-block

219

Two-handed Grasping Block

Side Combined Block

Reverse Wedge Block   **Reverse Wedge Block (open hand)**

● *Important Points*

1. If a punch is directed at your head by an opponent standing at your left, shift your feet into the back stance and face the direction of the attack. At the same time, cross your wrists at your right hip and bring your hands up to deflect the punch. Your block should contact the opponent's wrist slightly in front of and above your left shoulder.

2. It is possible to block the attack with the right hand alone, but the block is stronger when supported by the left. Strongly press the backs of your right hand with the back of your left as the hands move from your hip to your shoulder.

● *Morote-tsukami-uke* (*two-handed grasping block*)

This technique is an effective block against a punch to your chest or solar plexus. As the opponent's right fist moves toward you, step to the rear with your right foot, push his forearm aside and then grasp it with your left hand, and grasp his wrist from above with your right. Force the opponent to continue his forward movement by pulling his arm toward your right side.

● *Important Points*

1. This block may fail if you are overly concerned with grasping the opponent's arm. Concentrate instead on changing the course of the attack.

2. In the situation described above, the left hand acts first to push the attacking forearm to the side and then to grasp it. The left hand must receive immediate reinforcement from the right, which grasps the attacking wrist from above.

3. As your left hand holds the attacking forearm, slide your right hand down the forearm to grasp the wrist and exert a pull to unbalance the opponent.

● *Kakiwake-uke* (*reverse wedge block*)

When the opponent attempts to choke you or has grasped your lapels with both hands, this block is an effective means of escape. Thrust both hands upward between the opponent's wrists until your wrists are crossed in front of your face. Then force your forearms downward and outward to the sides, forcing the opponent's arms apart. This block can be done with either open hands or fists.

● *Important Points*

1. After thrusting your hands between the opponent's arms, drop your body downward to the rear by taking a step backward and lowering your hips. At the same time, force your forearms downward and twist them outward to both sides.

2. As you force your forearms downward, direct your elbows toward your sides and tense the muscles around your armpits. Simultaneously, use your hands to apply strong outward pressure to force the opponent's forearms apart.

Downward Hooking Block (from outside)

Downward Hooking Block (from inside)

Blocking Techniques Against Kicks

Gedan-kake-uke (*downward hooking block*)

To perform the downward hooking block, swing your arm downward in a large circle, striking and hooking the opponent's kicking leg upward at the ankle. This block can be done in two ways. One method is swinging the arm from the outside inward and the other is swinging the arm from the inside outward.

● *Important Points*

1. As the opponent's kick moves toward you, take a step to the rear into the front stance at *hanmi*. If you swing your arm from the outside inward, step to the rear with the leg opposite your blocking arm. On the other hand, if you block from the inside outward, step to the rear with the leg on the same side of the body as your blocking arm.

2. When blocking, the portion of your wrist above the thumb should contact the opponent's ankle. When you hook from the outside inward, rotate the forearm until the back of your fist faces forward. The block from the inside outward ends with the back of your fist facing the rear.

● *Sukui-uke* (*scooping block*)

The scooping block is a technique very similar to the downward hooking block. The major difference is that the opponent's ankle is caught with the open hand and then is pulled and lifted in this block. The scooping block can be applied either from the outside inward or from the inside outward.

● *Important Points*

1. As with the downward hooking block, begin this block by retreating one step from the natural position to the front stance at *hanmi*. When blocking from the

Scooping Block (from outside) **Scooping Block (from inside)** **Scooping Block (both hands)**

outside inward, withdraw the leg on the side of the body opposite the blocking arm. In the scooping block from the inside outward, step backward with the leg on the same side of the body as your blocking arm. To develop additional blocking power, coordinate your arm movement with the rotation of your hips.

2. Rotate the right forearm clockwise when scooping up from the outside inward, and rotate it counterclockwise when blocking from the inside outward.

3. As the opponent's kick approaches, extend your hand far forward to contact his leg near the calf. Then slide your hand to his ankle and scoop his leg upward.

4. Slightly crook the fingers and the palm of your blocking hand in order to facilitate scooping.

● *Morote-sukui-uke* (*two-handed scooping block*)

This block is done by applying the scooping block from the outside inward with one hand, while simultaneously pressing the opponent's knee with the other.

● *Important Points*

1. Squeeze the opponent's knee tightly between your thumb and fingers, and press the knee downward. The object of this pressure is to prevent the knee from bending and the foot from withdrawing.

2. Pull the hand scooping the opponent's ankle toward you and push his knee away from you. Withdraw the pulling hand below the elbow of the pushing arm.

Combined Palm-heel Block

Circular Sole Block

● *Teishō-awase-uke* (*combined palm-heel block*)
Place the heels of your hands together and thrust them strongly forward to block the opponent's kick.
● *Important Points*
1. Because kicks are usually powerful, drive your hips strongly forward as you block, and meet the kick with your feet firmly on the ground.
2. Bend your hands fully upward at the wrists and press the heels of the hands tightly together.
3. The combined palm-heel block will be ineffective unless you stop the opponent's kick before his leg is fully extended. Thus correct timing is very important.
● *Sokutei-mawashi-uke* (*circular sole block*)
Use the circular sole block technique against an attack to your solar plexus or abdomen. Swing your foot from the outside inward and sweep the opponent's forearm aside with the sole. Because it is unexpected, this block can be effective. This technique is especially valuable in a situation where the hands are unable to block.
● *Important Points*
1. Raise the knee of your blocking leg as high as possible at the start of the block and swing the foot in a circle from the outside inward.
2. As you begin the circular blocking movement, bend your blocking foot upward at the ankle and direct the sole of the foot inward. The object is to strike the opponent's forearm powerfully with the bottom of your foot.
3. As you block, rotate your hips and pivot on your supporting leg. The side of your hip should face the opponent at the end of the movement.
4. End this blocking technique with your knee fully bent and your blocking foot drawn close to your body to maintain balance and to facilitate a counterattack.

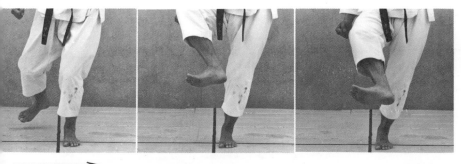

Pressing Block (with sole)

Pressing Block (with foot edge)

● *Sokutei-osae-uke* (*pressing block with sole*)
Use the pressing block with the sole to block the opponent's kick before it is fully launched. As the kick begins to move toward you, stop its advance by blocking and pressing the opponent's ankle with the sole of your foot.
● *Important Points*
   1.   Raise your blocking foot as high as the knee of your supporting leg and then drive it diagonally downward toward the advancing kick.
   2.   Fully bend the blocking foot upward at the ankle and turn your foot until the toes point outward to the side.
   3.   Thrust your hips forward when blocking, to ensure sufficient power to stop a strong kick.
● *Sokutō-osae-uke* (*pressing block with foot edge*)
This block is similar to the previous technique. The major difference between them is that in this block is done with the edge of the foot instead of with the sole.
● *Important Points*
   1.   As the opponent begins his kick, rotate your hips and turn 90 degrees on your supporting leg. Simultaneously, raise your knee and thrust the edge of your foot diagonally downward toward the opponent's ankle.
   2.   Fully bend your blocking foot upward at the ankle and point your toes inward until the edge of your foot points toward the opponent.

● *Ashibō-kake-uke* (*leg hooking block*)

Use this technique to block the opponent's side-thrust kick to your abdomen. Raise your leg to the side and swing it in a circle designed to deflect the opponent's kick.

● *Important Points*

1. Raise your knee high and bend it as you swing your leg around to deflect the opponent's kick. Block the back of the opponent's ankle with your shin. After blocking, pull your leg close to your body by fully bending your knee.

2. Bend the foot of your blocking leg inward until the edge of the foot is directed toward the ground. Tighten the foot and ankle.

3. Increase the power in your block by rotating your hips and pivoting in the direction taken by your blocking leg.

● *Ashikubi-kake-uke* (*ankle hooking block*)

This technique is designed to block an opponent's front kick by hooking it upward and forward. Use the front of your ankle to hook his leg below the calf.

● *Important Points*

1. As the opponent starts his kick, begin to swing your foot toward him from the side. Contact the opponent's kicking leg by hooking the area below his calf with the front of your ankle. Raise your foot high and draw it toward your body, pulling the opponent's leg up and forward.

2. To facilitate hooking the opponent's leg, point your blocking foot inward and bend it upward toward your ankle.

3. As you apply this blocking technique, rotate your hips and pivot on the supporting leg. End the block by drawing the ankle of your blocking leg close to your body.

The author (center) countering attacks from two sides simultaneously.

7. Basic Training in Blocking Techniques

Stand face-to-face with a partner, close enough to enable you to reach him with your extended fist without leaning forward. Practice the following blocking techniques. Partner "A" and "B" must switch roles after each practice set.

"A"	"B"
1. Right punch to face ·············→	Left upper block
2. Left upper block ←·················	Right punch to face
3. Right punch to body ·············→	Left forearm block from outside inward
4. Left forearm block from outside inward ·················	Right punch to body
5. Right punch to groin ·············→	Left downward block
6. Left downward block ·············	Right punch to groin

Continue with the following:

1. Right punch to face ·············→	Right upper block
2. Left upper block ←·········	Left punch to face
3. Right punch to body ·············→	Right forearm block from outside inward
4. Left forearm block ←······ from outside inward	Left punch to body
5. Right punch to groin ·············→	Right downward block
6. Left downward block ←·············	Left punch to groin

Practice blocking punch to body with forearm blocks from inside outward and from outside inward. Perform the complete series of attacks and blocks slowly at first, gradually adding speed and power as you grow more proficient.

Part III
The Application of
Fundamental Techniques

◀ Instructor T. Mikami (left) drives in to attack as T. Asai prepares for a counter in the semi-finals of the 7th Annual Karate Championship.

Chapter 9
Defense and Countering Jōdan (Upper) Attacks

Upper Block to Reverse Punch (ordinary distance)

**Upper Block to Upward
Elbow Strike (close range)**

Counterattacks from the Upper Block 1

Upper Block to Forward Elbow Strike (close range)

Upper Block to Side-round Elbow Strike (close range)

**Upper Block to Round Kick
(relatively far apart in hanmi)**

Upper Block to Front Kick (relatively far apart)

Upper Block to Front Snap Kick (relatively close range)

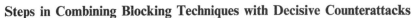

Steps in Combining Blocking Techniques with Decisive Counterattacks

1. Begin by prearranging the specific techniques you will use to block and counter your partner's attack. This formal method of practicing is a necessary preliminary to more advanced practice.

2. As in #1 above, prearrange your response to your partner's attack, but concentrate on improving your timing and speed in the shift from block to counterattack. Emphasize speed and coordination.

3. After attaining proficiency in the method suggested in #2, it is no longer necessary to choose your counterattack in advance. Instead, at the instant you block, base your choice of counter on your stance and on your position in relation to that of your opponent. For example, if your block is late, select a counter technique which lends itself to a delivery of above average speed. Learn to make split-second decisions of this kind.

● *Important Considerations*

1. Position of Eyes—Keep your eyes on the center of the triangle formed by the opponent's shoulders and eyes. If you concentrate on his hands or feet, you may become confused or distracted.

2. Movement of Feet—Move your feet lightly and quickly. Slide smoothly over the ground. When stepping forward be sure also to thrust your hips forward.

3. State of Mind—Avoid showing fear when the opponent attacks. Apply your techniques with confidence.

4. Application of Power—Be prepared to focus all available power whenever necessary. After it has served its purpose, instantly release the tension.

Practice each technique repeatedly, sometimes stepping forward and sometimes to the rear. Your body will gradually grow accustomed to the required movements.

Counterattacks from the Upper Block 2

Upper Block to Roundhouse Punch (ordinary distance)

Upper Block to Round Kick (relatively far apart)

Upper Block to Elbow Strike
(close range, stepping in)

Counterattacks from the Upper Block 3

Upper Block to Back-fist Strike (relatively close range)

Counterattacks from the Upper Block 4

Upper Block to Forward Elbow Strike (close range)

Upper Block to Front Kick (relatively far apart)

Upper Block to Round Kick (relatively far apart)

Counterattacks from the Forearm Block

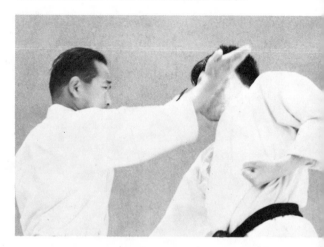

Forearm Block against head attack to Side Snap Kick (relatively far apart, with body facing the side).

Forearm Block against head attack to Round Kick

Forearm Block against head attack to Side Elbow Strike (relatively close range)

Forearm Block against head attack to Upward Back-fist Strike (relatively close range)

239

Forearm Block to Hook Punch (close range)

←

↓

Forearm Block against head attack to Fist-hammer Strike with blocking hand (slightly closer than ordinary distance)

↓

Forearm Block against head attack to Punch with blocking hand (ordinary distance)

Counterattacks from the Sweeping Block

Elbow Strike (close range)

Spear-hand (ordinary distance)

**Close Punch
(relatively close range)**

Vertical Spear-hand (ordinary distance)

Punch (ordinary distance)

Counterattacks from the Back-arm Block

Back-arm Block to Close Punch (slightly closer than ordinary distance)

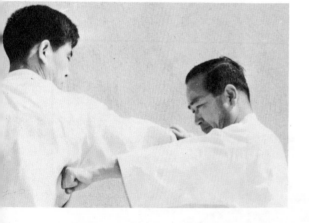

Back-arm Block to Reverse Punch (ordinary distance)

Back-arm Block to Close Punch with blocking arm (ordinary distance, facing side)

Back-arm Block to Straight Punch

Back-arm Block to Round Kick (relatively far apart)

Counterattacks from the X-block

X-block against head attack to Circular Knife-hand Strike from inside outward (ordinary distance)

Fist-hammer Strike (ordinary distance)

X-block against head attack to Circular Knife-hand Strike from outside inward (ordinary distance)

X-block against head attack to Reverse Knife-hand Strike (ordinary distance) (upper right); Ox-jaw Hand Strike (ordinary distance)

X-block against head attack to Front Kick (relatively far apart)

Counterattacks from the Side-combined Block

Side-Combined Block against head attack to Front Kick (ordinary distance) (upper right); Round Kick (ordinary distance) (lower right)

The author (left) displays a fine example of nukite, brushing Instructor H. Kanazawa's elbow to deflect his punch and score with a stab to the eye.

Chapter 10

Defense and Countering Chūdan (Mid-Section) Attacks

Counterattacks from the
Inside Outward Forearm Block

Block from outside in-
ward with bottom of
wrist to Punch with
blocking arm
(ordinary distance)

Block from outside inward with bottom
of wrist to Back-fist Strike (slightly
closer than ordinary distance)

Block from outside inward with bottom of wrist to Reverse Punch (ordinary distance)

Block from outside inward with bottom of wrist to Elbow Strike (closer than ordinary distance)

Block from outside inward with bottom of wrist to Elbow Strike (closer than ordinary distance)

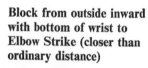

Block from outside inward with bottom of wrist to Elbow Strike (closer than ordinary distance)

Counterattacks from the Outside Inward Forearm Block

Block from inside outward with top of wrist to Punch (ordinary distance)

Block from inside outward with top of wrist and hand support to Close Punch (slightly closer than ordinary distance)

Block from inside outward to Punch (ordinary distance)

Block from inside outward to Roundhouse Punch (ordinary distance)

Counterattacks from the Hooking Block

Hooking Block to Side Thrust Kick (relatively far apart with body facing side)

Hooking Block to Punch (slightly apart than ordinary distance)

**Hooking Block to Round Kick
(slightly more than ordi-
nary distance)**

Side Thrust Kick

Counterattacks from the Knife-hand Block

Knife-hand Block to Vertical Spear-hand (ordinary distance)

**Knife-hand Block to Front Snap Kick
(ordinary distance)**

**Knife-hand Block to Circular Knife-
hand Strike (ordinary distance)**

**Knife-hand Block to Horizontal
Spear-hand (ordinary distance)**

Attack to ribs with Horizontal Spear-hand

Knife-hand Block to Spear-hand with blocking hand

Counterattacks from Other Blocks

Two-handed Grasping Block to (a) Front Kick and (b) Round Kick (slightly apart)

Reverse Wedge Block to Front Kick (ordinary distance)

256

→ **Dropping Block to (a) Back-fist Strike and (b) Knife-hand Strike (slightly closer than ordinary distance)**

Dropping Block to Reverse Punch (ordinary distance)

Palm-heel Block to Bent-wrist Strike (slightly close range)

257

Hand Pressing Block to Reverse Punch (ordinary distance)

Wrist-hook Block to Palm-heel Strike (slightly closer than ordinary distance)

Wrist-hook Block to Palm-heel Strike with blocking arm (close range)

Instructor S. Miyazaki (right) steps in to counter with uraken sidestepping A. Takahashi's kick.

Chapter 11

Defense and Countering Gedan (Lower) Attacks

Knife-hand Downward Block to Knife-hand Strike

Counterattacks from Two-handed Blocks

Combined Palm-heel Block to Elbow Strike →

Counterattacks from the Downward Block

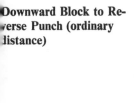

Downward Block to Reverse Punch (ordinary distance)

Downward Block to Round Kick (slightly apart)

X-block against lower body attack to Front Kick (ordinary distance)

261

**Scooping Block from inside outward to Front Kick
(further apart than ordinary distance)**

Scooping Block from outside inward to Punch (ordinary distance)

Circular Sole Block to Side Thrust Kick (apart than ordinary distance)

Counterattacks from Other Blocks

Two-handed Scooping Block to Two-handed Punch to shin

Pressing Block with foot edge to Back-fist Strike (slightly close range)

→ **Pressing Block with sole to Round Kick (slightly apart)**

→ **Leg-hooking Block to Side Thrust Kick (ordinary distance)**

Part IV
Completion of
Fundamental Techniques

Instructor H. Shirai (right) scores with a kick as K. Enoeda blocks a fraction too late with gedan-barai in the 1963 Kyushu Championships.

Chapter 12

Basic Training

Training in individual techniques can take the form of consecutive forward or rearward steps. For instance, lunge punch practice is usually done by repeating the technique in five separate forward steps, turning, and again punching and stepping five times in the opposite direction. This practice can be repeated endlessly. Pause after each movement to be sure your stance is strong and well balanced and that your attack is correctly aimed. Training in consecutive rearward movements is especially important in the case of blocking techniques.

After attaining some proficiency in the performance of individual techniques, begin training for the application of combination techniques. For example, the upper block might be followed by a reverse punch.

When practicing combination techniques, move from one technique to the next with maximum speed. However, your techniques will be ineffective, and your training of little value, if you sacrifice power and correctness of form for quick execution. For example, it is obvious that a stable, strong stance is required for the delivery of effective offensive or defensive techniques. Yet, students appear to ignore this fact when they try to move too quickly from one technique to the next. Work slowly at first. As your skill increases, gradually increase the speed of your techniques and reduce the interval of time between them.

Another important point in combination techniques concerns the use of the hips. If you move from one technique to the next too quickly to allow proper hip rotation, your techniques will be weak. Moreover, it has been demonstrated that when the hips are fully rotated in one direction, they automatically tend to rotate in the reverse direction. Utilize this reaction to increase the effect of the follow-up technique. For instance, use hip rotation when moving from the round kick to the back-fist strike. Delivered in this way, the back-fist strike will be more powerful than if individually applied.

Oi-zuki (lunge punch)

A. Assume the downward block position with your body at *hanmi*.

B. Step forward and deliver the lunge punch with your right arm.

C. Advance a step and deliver another lunge punch with your left arm.

D. Continue advancing until you have completed a total of four steps and four alternate punches.

E. Upon completion of the fourth step, turn around by shifting your rear foot to the left and pivoting on your front foot. Assume the downward block position at *hanmi*.

F. Advance in the opposite direction and practice the lunge punch in the same manner described above. Continue this sequence as many times as desired.

G. It is also necessary to practice the lunge punch while retreating.

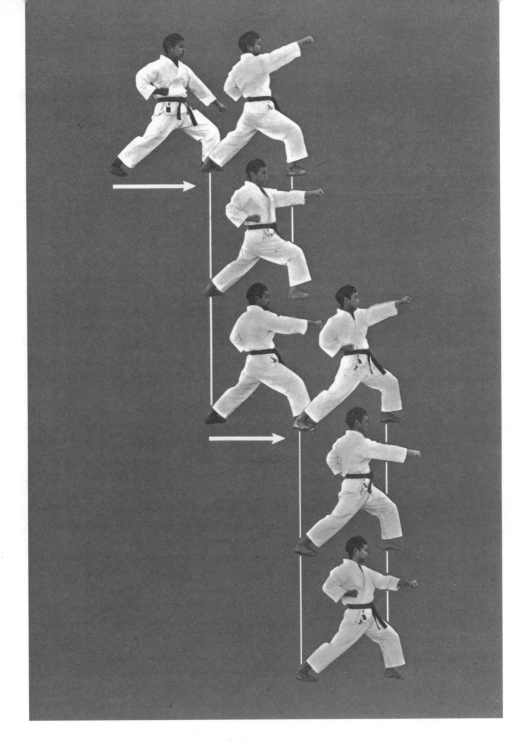

Sanren-zuki (three consecutive punches)

A. Assume the downward block position with your body at *hanmi*.

B. Step forward and deliver three consecutive punches composed of a right lunge punch to the face, a left reverse punch to the body, and a right lunge punch to the body. Deliver the first punch at the end of the forward step and the next two punches without shifting the feet.

C. Continue advancing and throwing three consecutive punches at the end of each step until you have completed four or five steps.

D. Upon completion of the last step, turn around. Practice the sequence of steps and three consecutive punches in the opposite direction.

E. It is also necessary to practice three consecutive punches while retreating.

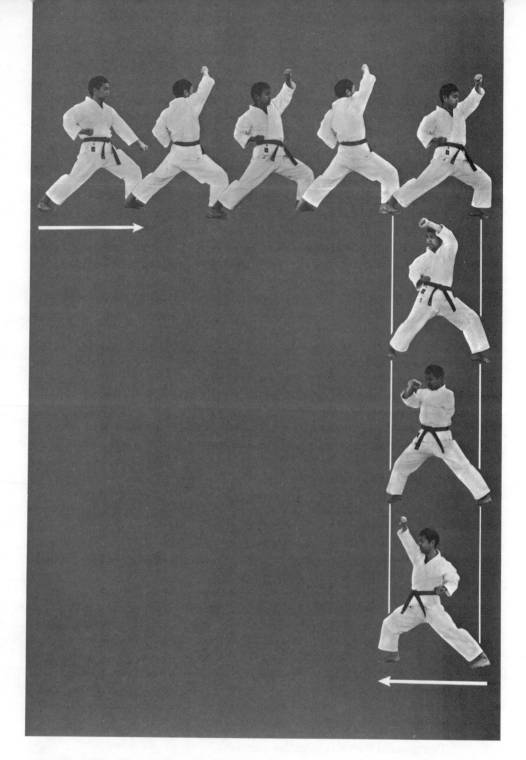

Age-uke (upper block)

    A. Assume the downward block position at *hanmi*.

    B. Step forward and deliver the upper block.

    C. Continue advancing until you have completed four consecutive steps and four blocks.

    D. Turn around and assume the upper block position at *hanmi*.

    E. Resume your practice by advancing four steps in the opposite direction.

Age-uke (upper block) to Gyaku-zuki (reverse punch)

A. Assume the downward block position at *hanmi*.

B. Take a step backward and deliver an upper block followed immediately by a reverse punch.

C. Continue retreating until you have completed four consecutive steps with the upper block and reverse punch.

D. Turn in the opposite direction by pivoting on your right foot. Assume the left upper block position and follow up with a right reverse punch.

E. Resume your practice by retreating four steps in the opposite direction.

Chūdan-ude-uke (forearm block against body attack)

   A. Assume the downward block position at *hanmi*.

   B. Take four consecutive forward steps, executing a forearm block at the end of each step.

   C. Turn in the opposite direction and repeat the movements in **B**.

Chūdan-ude-uke (forearm block against body attack) to Gyaku-zuki (reverse punch)

A. Step backward and perform a forearm block followed immediately by a reverse punch.

B. Follow the procedure used in upper block to reverse punch. Perform a forearm block and a reverse punch at the end of each of four rearward steps, turn around, and repeat the movements while retreating four steps in the opposite direction.

Ude-uke (forearm block) to Empi-uchi (elbow strike)
    A.   Assume the downward block position at *hanmi*.
    B.   Step forward and deliver a forearm block.
    C.   Shift to the straddle-leg stance and apply the elbow strike.
    D.   Continue alternate blocks and counters, stepping forward each time you apply a forearm block and move to the straddle-leg stance when you apply the elbow strike. Whenever you practice blocking techniques be sure to perform the block while retreating as well as while advancing.

Shutō-uke (knife-hand block), Retreating

    A.   Assume the downward block position at *hanmi*.

    B.   Step back into the left-back stance and deliver a right knife-hand block.

    C.   Retreat another step and deliver a left knife-hand block.

    D.   Continue retreating while alternately delivering right and left knife-hand blocks until you have completed a total of four steps.

    E.   Pivot on your left foot, turn around, and assume the left-back stance and a right knife-hand block.

    F.   Continue your practice while retreating in the opposite direction.

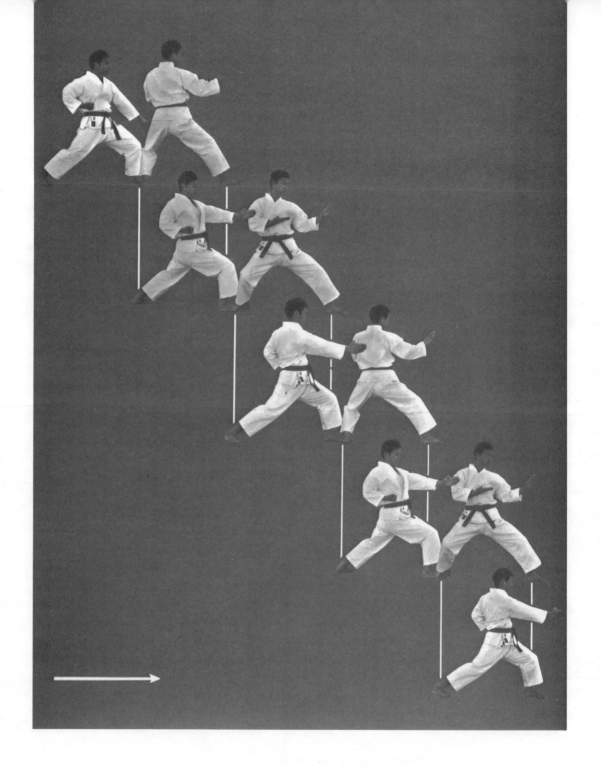

Shutō-uke (knife-hand block) to Nukite (spear-hand)

A. Step forward into the left-back stance and apply a right knife-hand block.

B. Shift your center of gravity forward, change your stance to the right-front stance, and deliver the spear-hand attack with your left hand.

C. Continue advancing with alternate blocks and counters, stepping forward into the back stance to apply the knife-hand block, and shifting into the front stance to apply the spear-hand attack.

NOTES:
- Techniques which are applied from the back stance must also be practiced as you step backward into this stance. In fact, you should devote more attention to retreating than to advancing in the back stance.
- After completing the required number of steps in one direction, turn around by smoothly rotating your hips and by shifting your center of gravity.
- Most blocks are done with the body in *hanmi*. When you counter with a reverse punch or a spear-hand, be sure to rotate your hips from *hanmi* until they face squarely forward.
- When, after applying a block from a front or back stance, you shift to the straddle-leg stance in order to counter with a back-fist strike or an elbow strike, concentrate on correctly rotating your hips. Simultaneously, shift both feet into the correct position for the straddle-leg stance.
- When practicing a combination block and counterattack, the same arm that applied the counter must apply the block in the next move. For example, in combining an upper block with a reverse punch, the same arm used for the reverse punch is used for the upper block to follow. Thus, if your first step consists of a left upper block and a right reverse punch, your next move will be the right upper block.
- Clearly demonstrate muscular tension and relaxation as you practice. Concentrate all your power at the moment of impact, but between moments of tension move in a loose and relaxed manner.

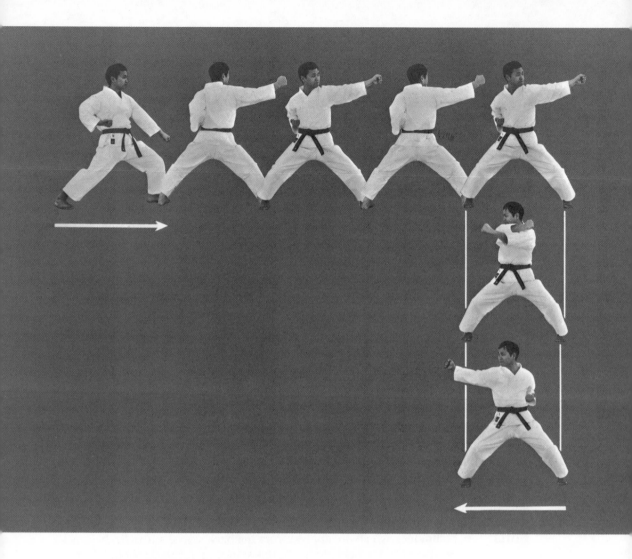

Uraken-uchi (back-fist strike)

A. Assume the downward block position at *hanmi*.

B. Step forward from the front stance to the straddle-leg stance and deliver a back-fist strike.

C. Continue shifting your position as shown in the photos until you have completed the required number of back-fist strikes.

Kizami-zuki (jab) to Oi-zuki (lunge punch) to Uraken-uchi (back-fist strike) to Shutō-soto-mawashi-uchi (circular knife-hand strike from outside inward) to Shutō-uchi-mawashi-uchi (circular knife-hand strike from inside outward)

A. Assume a ready position with the right foot forward and then deliver a right jab.

B. Immediately step forward with the rear foot and deliver a left lunge punch.

C. Step forward again, face the side, assume the straddle-leg stance, and deliver a right back-fist strike.

D. Step forward with the left foot to the left-front stance and deliver a circular knife-hand strike by rotating your left arm in a big circle from the outside inward to the target.

E. Without changing your stance, deliver another circular knife-hand strike by snapping your left hand from the inside outward to the target.

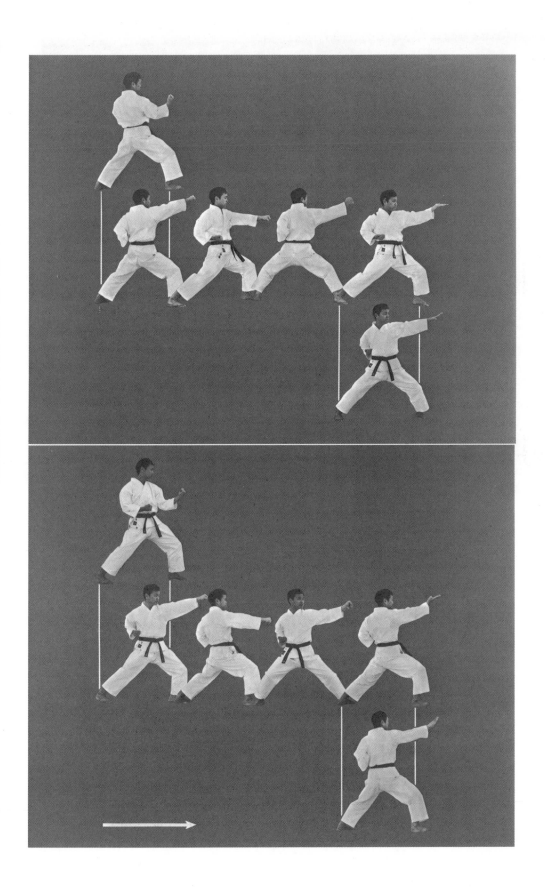

Mae-geri (front kick), Advancing

A. Assume the left-front stance.

B. Snap the right foot outward toward the target with a front kick, snap it back to the height of the left knee, and then return it to the floor as you move forward into the right-front stance.

C. From the right-front stance, apply a left-front kick and advance.

D. Repeat front kicks alternately for a total of four kicks and then turn.

Mawashi-geri (round kick)

A. Assume the right-front stance.

B. Deliver a round kick with a snap of the left foot, withdraw the foot to the height of the right knee, and then step forward into the left-front stance.

C. Repeat the same kick using the right leg.

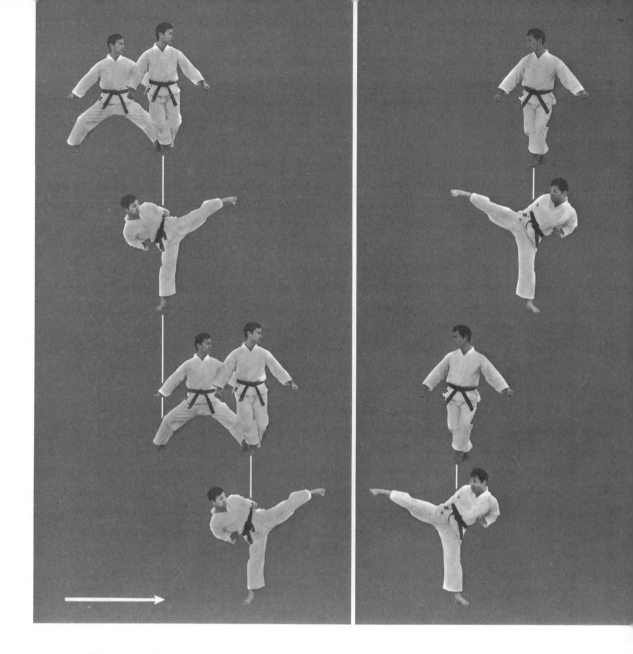

Yoko-geri (side kick)

A. Assume the straddle-leg stance.

B. Slide the right foot toward the left and step across the left. At this point the outer edges of both feet should be touching.

C. Shift the center of gravity completely to your right leg, raise your left foot from behind your right leg, and deliver a side kick.

D. Practice side kicks for two counts, first in one direction and then in the other.

E. The side kick practice includes both the snap kick and the thrust kick.

Mae-geri (front kick) to Mawashi-geri (round kick) to Yoko-geri-keage (side snap kick) or Yoko-geri-kekomi (side thrust kick)

A.   Assume the left-front stance. Deliver a front kick with the right leg.

B.   Withdraw the right foot to the height of the left knee and then to the ground as you step forward into the right-front stance.

C.   As soon as you are in the right-front stance, deliver a round kick with the left leg. Return the kicking foot to the ground as you step forward into the left-front stance.

D.   Rotate your hips and apply a side snap kick or thrust kick with the right leg to a target directly ahead. Bring the leg to the ground as you step forward into the right-front stance.

E.   Reverse your feet, change your stance to the left-front stance and resume the sequence above.

Age-uke (upper block) to Mawashi-geri (round kick) to Uraken-uchi (back-fist strike) to Oi-zuki (lunge punch)

A. Assume the left-front stance. Move forward into the right-front stance and apply an upper block.

B. Immediately deliver a round kick with the left foot.

C. Bring the kicking foot to the ground and shift into the straddle-leg stance. As soon as your foot touches the ground snap your hand outward to the side in a back-fist strike.

D. Immediately step forward and deliver a right lunge punch.

E. Practice these movements also by beginning in a tight front stance and performing the technique on the opposite side of the body.

F. It is perhaps even more important to practice the above technique while stepping to the rear.

Mawashi-geri (round kick) to Yoko-geri-kekomi (side thrust kick) or Yoko-geri-keage (side snap kick)

A.   Assume the right-front stance in the ready position. Apply a round kick with the left foot.

B.   Bring your kicking foot to the ground and shift into the left-front stance. Immediately deliver a side thrust kick with your right leg.

C.   Bring your right foot to the ground as you assume the right-front stance. Step forward into the left-front stance and repeat the sequence on the opposite side of the body.

Mae-geri (front kick) or Mawashi-geri (round kick) to Yoko-geri-kekomi (side thrust kick) or Keage (side snap kick)

A.   Assume a ready position with the right foot advanced. Deliver a front kick with the left foot.

B.   Withdraw the kicking foot to the height of your right knee, rotate your hips clockwise, and again drive the foot to the target with a side thrust kick.

C.   Advance one step and repeat the practice with the right leg.

NOTE: In combination kicks your techniques will lack effectiveness if you fail to rotate your hips as you deliver the consecutive kicks. Before launching the second kick, be sure to withdraw the kicking foot to knee level of the supporting leg. As you shift from one kick to the next, smoothly adjust the position of your center of gravity and concentrate on maintaining good balance.

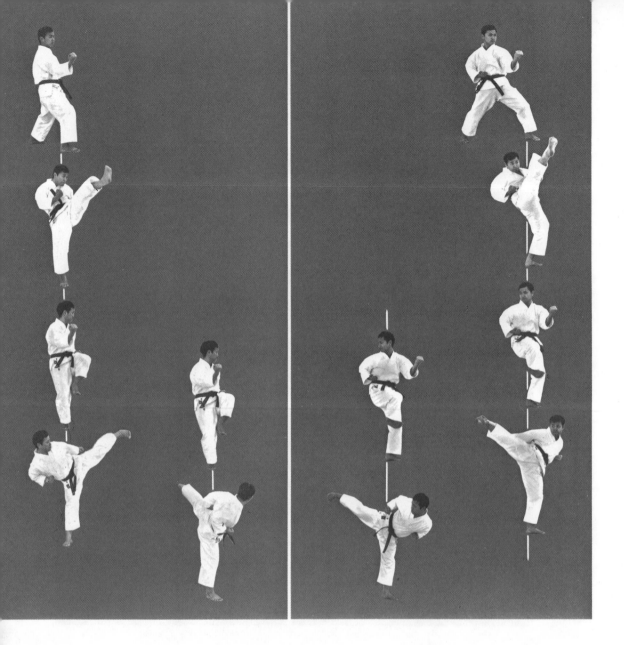

Mae-geri (front kick) to Yoko-geri (side kick) to Ushiro-geri (back kick)

A. Assume the right-front stance in the ready position.

B. Apply a front kick with the left leg.

C. Return the kicking foot to the knee of the supporting leg and then apply a side kick to the side.

D. Again return the kicking foot to the supporting leg and kick to the rear with a back kick.

E. Reverse the position of the feet and practice the sequence of kicks with your right leg.

NOTE: Throughout this practice maintain good balance, tighten the ankle and the knee of the supporting leg, and thrust your hips in the direction of each kick.

SHIHO-WARI
Demonstration of power by breaking boards held in four different directions using the Empi-uchi, Yoko-geri, Shutō-uchi, and Choku-zuki, by Instructor H. Kanazawa.

Chapter 13

Calisthenics and Exercises

Calisthenics

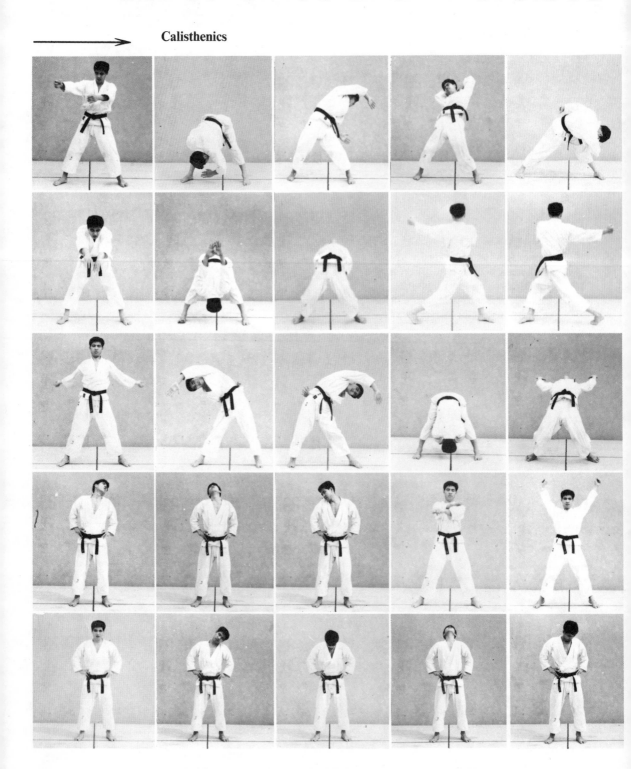

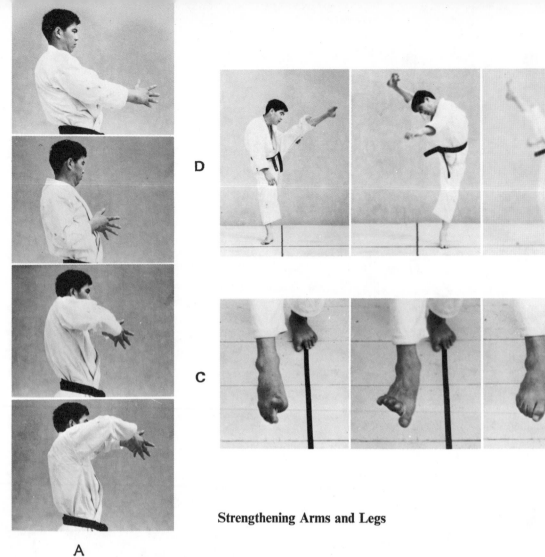

D

C

A

B

Strengthening Arms and Legs

A.   Increasing wrist strength and flexibility.
B.   Increasing gripping power.
C.   Increasing toe control.
D.   Increasing leg flexibility.
E.   Strengthening arms and wrists with push-ups.
F-1.   Stretching inner thigh.
F-2.   Strengthening toes and stretching inner thigh.
G.   Strengthening shoulders, arms, and wrists using heavy club.

E

G

F–1

F–2

Two-man Training for Power and Flexibility

Use of the Sandbag

Use of the Makiwara (punching board)

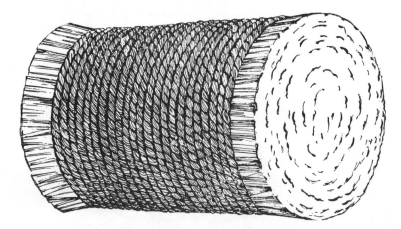

Hanging Makiwara
(length, approx. 24 inches;
diameter, approx. 12 inches)

How to Make a Makiwara

Standing Makiwara
(thickness of the board at top: 3/4 inch;
thickness at bottom. 3-1/2 inches; width: 4 inches)

Makiwara
(length, approx. 15 inches;
width, 4 to 4-1/2 inches)

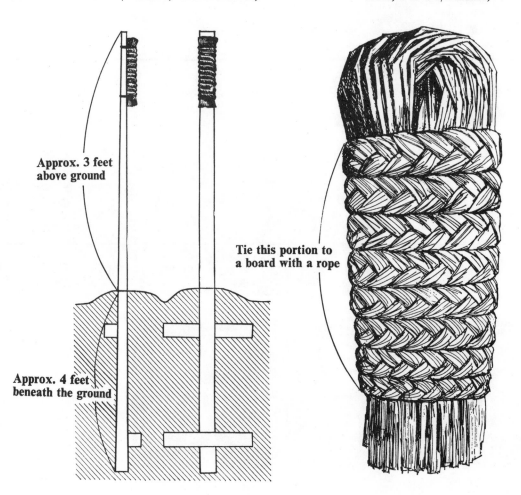

Approx. 3 feet
above ground

Tie this portion to
a board with a rope

Approx. 4 feet
beneath the ground

Other Necessary Equipment

**Substitute for Makiwara
(made of felt)**

**Iron clogs
(worn to strengthen legs)**

Wooden club

**Iron hand-grip
(used to strengthen hands)
(Barbells and Expanders are also used)**

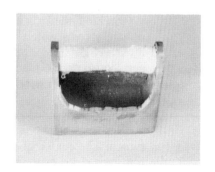

Appendices

An Analysis of Karate Movements

Presented here are some experimental analyses of karate movements, obtained by the author in collaboration with Professor Yoshio Kato of Takushoku University, Tokyo. Electromyograms were taken and a 16 mm motion picture camera was used to film (64 frames per second) muscle reactions and movements in karate.

I. a. Speed of a Straight Punch

Performer	Time required	Average speed	Maximum speed	Terminal speed
N fourth-dan	0.156	5.06m/sec.	7.10m/sec.	5.16m/sec.
S second-dan	0.219	3.25	6.71	4.48
M eighth-kyū	0.219	2.88	4.68	2.90

I. b. Speed of a Lunge Punch

Performer	Time required	Average speed	Maximum speed	Terminal speed
N fourth-dan		5.52	12.64	8.21
S second-dan		5.84	11.45	7.78
M eighth-kyū		3.35	7.10	4.56

The data obtained indicates that the fist of an advanced karate student travels to the target with a greater speed than that of a student who has not undergone as much training. The body movement when throwing the lunge punch showed the same phenomenon. The maximum speed was always recorded in the latter half of the entire movement. Setting the time required for the entire movement at 100, twenty examples of the twenty-three experiments made indicated that the maximum speed was recorded at a point between 70 and 80.

I. c. The Acceleration of the Fist in the Straight Punch

Checking the acceleration of T's fist (second-dan) when throwing a straight punch, it was noted that a great acceleration occurred immediately after the movement started, followed immediately by a deceleration; then a second great acceleration took place when the arm was extended, followed by another deceleration. The first acceleration was recorded at 74 m/sec. and the second at 37 m/sec.

I. d. Force Recorded in *Tameshiwari*

Two suspended *tameshiwari* boards (weight 1.5 kg.) were broken by a straight punch. The center of gravity of the body moved 8.5 cm. forward. Not all of the films are clear, especially at the point at which the fist hits and breaks the board.

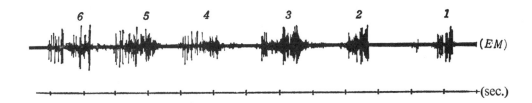

But, based on the clear films, an impact force of 170 kg./cm² was calculated, using an arbitrary contact time of 1/100 sec. However, in some of the films it was observed that the period of fist and board contact was clearly less than 1/64 sec. Thus, a contact time considerably less than 1/100 sec. is considered to be valid, resulting in a calculated impact force of even 700 kg./cm². (The subjects were photographed against a calibrated background of vertical white tapes strung at 10 cm. intervals. The films were shot from a distance of 8 m.)

II. Electromyograms of a Straight Punch

Following are some of the observations made of electromyograms obtained (two-volt D.C.; 1/100 sec.).

When throwing a straight punch, electric discharges were recorded from the extensor radiale in the forearm, the flexor radiale in the forearm, the triceps, and then the muscles on the side of the body in that order. This means that movement starts with the clenching of the fist, continues to the extension of the arm and then to the flexing of body muscles.

When the fist traveling to the target attained its maximum speed, the electromyogram showed a silent period or a recording positive to the silent period. This could be interpreted to mean either that to attain further speed, the muscles would be in danger of injury, or that communication from the brain or the impulse to throw the punch is controllable only to the point before the punch reaches maximum speed.

III. Observations of Electromyograms of Six Consecutive Straight Punches

The ordinary muscles contraction of the tricep in the upper arm shows a slow and gradual electric discharge when strength is exerted to pull or lift an object. In throwing a straight punch, however, the electric discharge recorded was abrupt and sudden, showing jagged oscillations (see illustration). When the punch movement ceased, the discharge did not linger, but also stopped abruptly, showing that as soon as the silent period is attained, the contraction of the muscles instantly turns to relaxation, a well-controlled function of the muscles. This indicates the result of the degree of training in karate.

In the first two of the six consecutive punches, the electromyograms show that the electric discharge generally follows the pattern described above. From the third punch, and after, however, the electric discharges were extended, indicating muscles fatigue (in quick movements). The above experiments were made with 150-gram weights attached to the forefinger.

Anatomical Charts of Human Musculature
Front

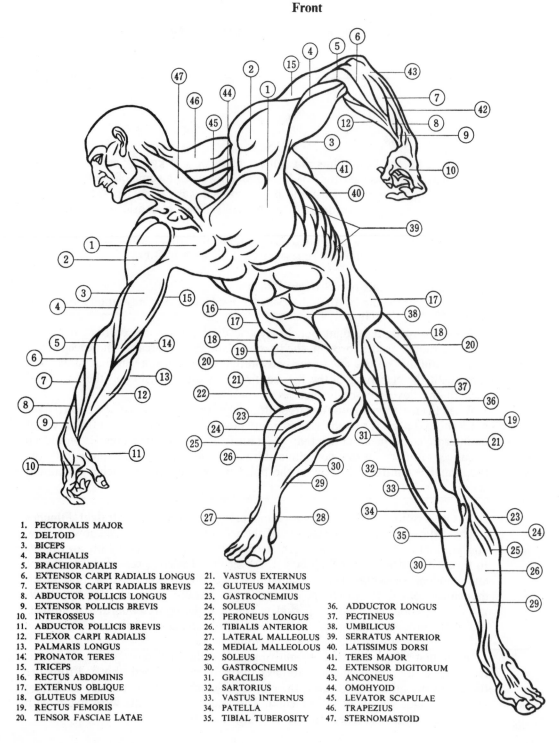

1. PECTORALIS MAJOR
2. DELTOID
3. BICEPS
4. BRACHIALIS
5. BRACHIORADIALIS
6. EXTENSOR CARPI RADIALIS LONGUS
7. EXTENSOR CARPI RADIALIS BREVIS
8. ABDUCTOR POLLICIS LONGUS
9. EXTENSOR POLLICIS BREVIS
10. INTEROSSEUS
11. ABDUCTOR POLLICIS BREVIS
12. FLEXOR CARPI RADIALIS
13. PALMARIS LONGUS
14. PRONATOR TERES
15. TRICEPS
16. RECTUS ABDOMINIS
17. EXTERNUS OBLIQUE
18. GLUTEUS MEDIUS
19. RECTUS FEMORIS
20. TENSOR FASCIAE LATAE

21. VASTUS EXTERNUS
22. GLUTEUS MAXIMUS
23. GASTROCNEMIUS
24. SOLEUS
25. PERONEUS LONGUS
26. TIBIALIS ANTERIOR
27. LATERAL MALLEOLUS
28. MEDIAL MALLEOLOUS
29. SOLEUS
30. GASTROCNEMIUS
31. GRACILIS
32. SARTORIUS
33. VASTUS INTERNUS
34. PATELLA
35. TIBIAL TUBEROSITY

36. ADDUCTOR LONGUS
37. PECTINEUS
38. UMBILICUS
39. SERRATUS ANTERIOR
40. LATISSIMUS DORSI
41. TERES MAJOR
42. EXTENSOR DIGITORUM
43. ANCONEUS
44. OMOHYOID
45. LEVATOR SCAPULAE
46. TRAPEZIUS
47. STERNOMASTOID

Back

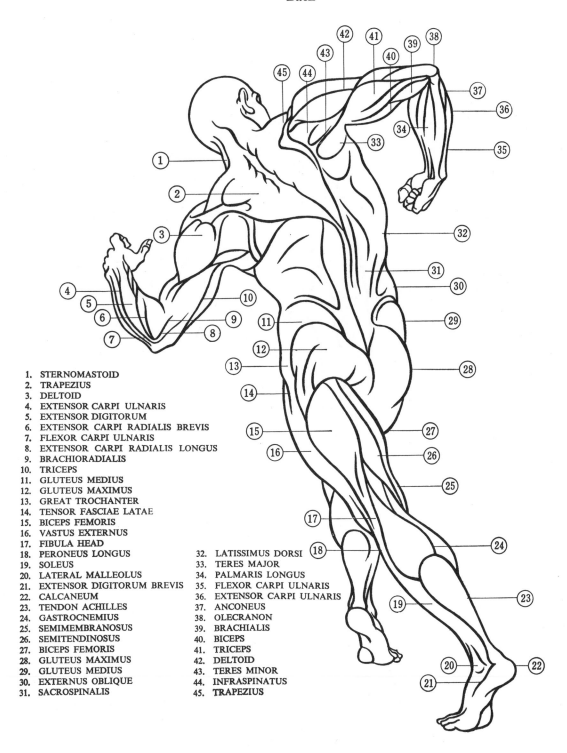

1. STERNOMASTOID
2. TRAPEZIUS
3. DELTOID
4. EXTENSOR CARPI ULNARIS
5. EXTENSOR DIGITORUM
6. EXTENSOR CARPI RADIALIS BREVIS
7. FLEXOR CARPI ULNARIS
8. EXTENSOR CARPI RADIALIS LONGUS
9. BRACHIORADIALIS
10. TRICEPS
11. GLUTEUS MEDIUS
12. GLUTEUS MAXIMUS
13. GREAT TROCHANTER
14. TENSOR FASCIAE LATAE
15. BICEPS FEMORIS
16. VASTUS EXTERNUS
17. FIBULA HEAD
18. PERONEUS LONGUS
19. SOLEUS
20. LATERAL MALLEOLUS
21. EXTENSOR DIGITORUM BREVIS
22. CALCANEUM
23. TENDON ACHILLES
24. GASTROCNEMIUS
25. SEMIMEMBRANOSUS
26. SEMITENDINOSUS
27. BICEPS FEMORIS
28. GLUTEUS MAXIMUS
29. GLUTEUS MEDIUS
30. EXTERNUS OBLIQUE
31. SACROSPINALIS

32. LATISSIMUS DORSI
33. TERES MAJOR
34. PALMARIS LONGUS
35. FLEXOR CARPI ULNARIS
36. EXTENSOR CARPI ULNARIS
37. ANCONEUS
38. OLECRANON
39. BRACHIALIS
40. BICEPS
41. TRICEPS
42. DELTOID
43. TERES MINOR
44. INFRASPINATUS
45. TRAPEZIUS

Vulnerable Points in the Human Body
Front

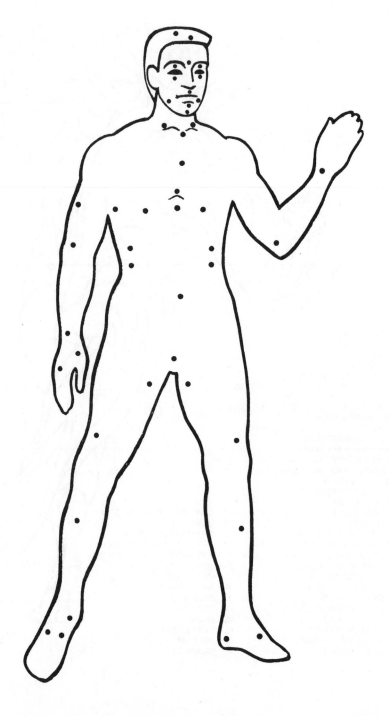

Back

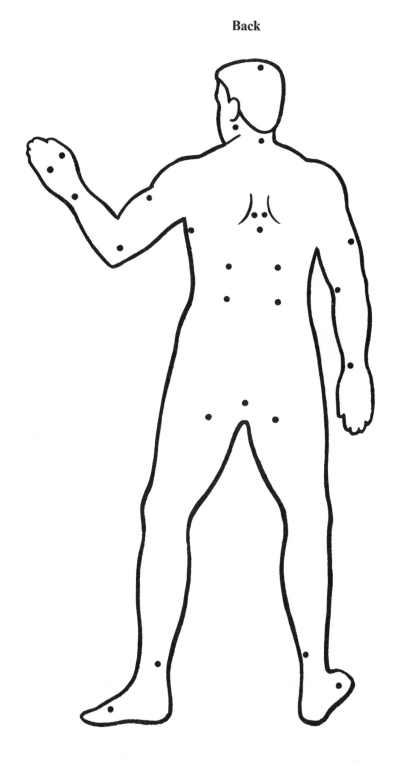

Glossary

Hai-wan (ha-ee wahn): Back-arm, 84

Haiwan-nagashi-uke (ha-ee-wahn nah-gah-she oo-kay): Back-arm sweeping block, 214, 215

Hangetsu-dachi (hahn-geh-tsue dah-chee): Half-moon stance, 28, 38

Hangetsu kata (hahn-geh-tsue kah-tah): Half-moon formal exercise, 38

Hanmi (hahn-me): Half-front-facing position, 60

Hasami zuki (hah-sah-me zoo-key): Scissors punch, 97

Heikō-dachi (hay-koh dah-chee): Parallel stance, 26, 30

Heikō-zuki (Hay-koh zoo-key): parallel punch, 94

Heisoku-dachi (hay-sow-koo dah-chee): Informal attention stance, 26, 29

Hidari (he-dah-rhee): Left

Hidari-shizen-tai (he-dah-rhee she-zen tah-ee): Left natural position, 31

Hidari-teiji-dachi (he-dah-rhee teh-gee dah-chee): Left T-stance, 31

Hiji (he-gee): Elbow, 84

Hiji-ate (he-gee ah-teh): Elbow strike, 124

Hiji-suri-uke (he-gee sue-rhee oo-kay): Elbow sliding block, 192, 194

Hiji-uchi (he-gee oo-chee): Elbow strike, 120

Hiraken (he-rah-ken): Fore-knuckle fist, 78

Hiraken-zuki (he-rah-ken zoo-key): Fore-knuckle-fist straight punch, 78

Hizagashira (he-zah-gah-she-rah): Knee cap, 87

Ippon-ken (eep-pone ken): One-knuckle fist, 77

Ippon-ken zuki (eep-pone ken zoo-key): One-knuckle-fist straight punch, 77

Jiyū-kumite (gee-you koo-me-teh): Free-style sparring, 40

Jōdan (joe-dahn): Face area

Jōdan-age-uke (joe-dahn ah-geh oo-kay): Upper block against head attack, 176, 177, 182, 190, 191. 196–198

Jōdan-choku-zuki (joe-dahn cho-koo zoo-key): Upper straight punch. 98

Jōdan-kekomi (joe-dahn kay-koh-me): Thrust kick to face, 155

Jōdan-mae-geri (joe-dahn mah-eh geh-rhee): Front kick to face, 137

Jō-sokutei (joe so-koo-teh-ee): Raised sole, 85

Jūji-uke (jew-gee oo-kay): X-block. 218, 219

Kagi-zuki (kah-ghee zoo-key): Hook punch, 95

Kaishō (kah-ee-show): Open hand, 79, 81

Kakato (kah-kah-toe): Heel, 86

Kake-shutō-uke (kah-kay shoe-toe oo-kay): Hooking knife-hand block, 210

Kake-uke (kah-kay oo-kay): Hooking block, 215

Kakiwake-uke (kah-key-wah-kay oo-kay): Reverse wedge block ,220. 221

Kakutō (kah-koo-toe): Bent-wrist, 82

Kakutō-uke (kah-koo-toe oo-kay): Bent-wrist block, 212, 213

Kankū (kahn-koo): ,"Viewing the sky" kata form, 8

Karate (kah-rah-teh): Empty-hand fighting

Kata (kah-tah): Forms

Keage (kay-ah-geh): Snap kick, 140, 141, 150, 151

Kebanashi (kay-bah-nah-she): Kick off (snap kick), 150

Keitō (kay-toe): Chicken-head wrist, 83

Keitō-uke (kay-toe oo-kay): Chicken-head-wrist block, 212, 213

Kekomi (kay-koh-me): Thrust kick, 140, 142, 148, 152, 153

Kendō (ken-doe): Sword fighting

Kentsui (ken-tsue-ee): Fist-hammer, 77

Kentsui-uchi (ken-tsue-ee oo-chee): Fist-hammer strike, 122

Keri (kay-rhee): Kicking, 136

Keri-waza (kay-rhee wha-zah): Kicking techniques, 136

Kesa-geri (keh-sah geh-rhee): Diagonal kick, 161

Kiba-dachi (key-bah dah-chee): Straddle-leg stance, 27, 35, 42, 43, 48

Kihon kumite (key-hone koo-me-teh): Basic sparring

Kizami-zuki (key-zah-me zoo-key): Jab, 119

Kōkutsu-dachi (koe-koo-tsu dah-chee): Back stance, 27, 34, 42, 43, 46, 53

Ko-shi (ko-she): Ball of the foot, 85

Kumade (koo-mah-deh): Bear-hand, 82

Kumite (koo-me-teh): Sparring

Ma-ai (mah-aye): Distancing

Mae-ashi-geri (mah-eh ah-she geh-rhee): Front leg kick, 147

Mae-empi-uchi (mah-eh en-pee oo-chee): Forward elbow strike, 125, 126

Mae-geri (mah-eh geh-rhee): Front kick, 137-139, 144, 149, 280, 282

Mae-geri-keage (mah-eh geh-rhee

Sukui-uke (sue-koo-ee oo-kay):
Scooping block, 222, 223
Tameshi-wari (tah-meh-she-wah-rhee): Test of technique's power, 287
Tanden (tahn-den): Navel
Tate-empi-uchi (tah-teh en-pee oo-chee): Upward elbow strike, 130
Tate-hiji-ate (tah-teh he-gee ah-teh): Upward elbow strike, 130
Tate-shutō-uke (tah-teh shoe-toe oo-kay): Vertical knife-hand block, 210
Tate-zuki (tah-teh zoo-key): Vertical-fist punch, 93
Teiji-dachi (teh-gee dah-chee): T stance, 26, 31
Teishō (tay-show): Palm-heel, 81
Teishō-awase-uke (tay-show ah-wah-say oo-kay): Combined palm-heel block, 224
Teishō-uchi (tay-sho oo-chee): Palm heel strike, 81
Teishō-uke (tay-show oo-kay): Palm heel block, 212, 213
Teishō-zuki (tay-show zoo-key): Palm-heel punch, 81
Tekubi-kake-uke (teh-koo-be kah-kay oo-kay): Wrist-hook block, 214, 215
Te-nagashi-uke (teh na-gah-she oo-kay): Hand sweeping block, 214, 215
Te-osae-uke (teh oh-sah-eh oo-kay): Hand pressing block, 214, 215
Tobi-keri (tow-be keh-rhee): Jump kick, 161
Tobi-yoko-geri (tow-be yoh-koh-geh-rhee): Jumping side kick, 161, 164
Tsukami-uke (tsue-kah-me oo-kay): Grasping block, 221
Tsuki (tsue-key): Punching, 89, 93
Tsuki-waza (tsue-key wah-zah): Punching techniques, 89
Tsumasaki (tsue-mah-sah-key): Tips of toes, 87
Uchi (oo-chee): Striking, 120
Uchi-hachiji-dachi (oo-chee ha-chee-gee dah-chee): Inverted open-leg stance, 26, 31
Uchi-uke (oo-chee oo-kay): Block from inside outward, 179, 183
Uchi-waza (oo-chee wah-zah): Striking techniques, 120

Ude (oo-day): Forearm
Ude-uke (oo-day oo-kay): Forearm block, 192
Uke (oo-kay): Blocking, 174
Uraken (oo-rah-ken): Back-fist, 76
Uraken-uchi (oo-rah-ken oo-chee): Back-fist strike, 35, 122, 278
Ura-zuki (oo-rah zoo-key): Close punch, 94
Ushiro (oo-she-row): Back, rear
Ushiro-ashi-geri (oo-she-row ah-she geh-rhee): Rear-leg kick, 144, 145
Ushiro-empi-uchi (oo-she-row en-pee oo-chee): Back elbow strike, 128
Ushiro-geri (oo-she-row geh-rhee): Back kick, 159, 160
Ushiro-hiji-ate (oo-she-row he-gee ah-teh): Back elbow strike, 128
Wan (wahn): Arm, 84
Wantō (wahn-toe): Arm sword, 84
Washide (wah-she-deh): Eagle hand, 83
Yama-zuki (yah-mah zoo-key) Wide U-punch, 95
Yoko (yoh-koh): Side
Yoko-empi-uchi (yoh-koh en-pee oo-chee): Side elbow strike, 127
Yoko-geri (yoh-koh geh-rhee): Side kick, 139, 150, 167, 168, 281
Yoko-geri-keage (yoh-koh geh-rhee kay-ah-geh): Side snap kick, 282, 284, 285
Yoko-geri-kekomi (yoh-koh geh-rhee kay-koh-me): Side thrust kick, 282, 284, 285
Yoko-hiji-ate (yoh-koh he-gee ah-teh): Side elbow strike, 127
Yoko-kekomi (yoh-koh keh-koh-me): Side thrust kick, 282
Yoko-mawashi-empi-uchi (yoh-koh mah-wah-she en-pee oo-chee): Side-round elbow strike, 129
Yoko-mawashi-hiji-ate (yoh-koh mah-wah-she he-gee ah-teh): Side-round elbow strike, 129
Yoko-tobi-geri (yoh-koh toe-be geh-rhee): Jumping side kick, 164
Zenkutsu-dachi (zen-koo-tsue dah-chee): Forward stance, 27, 32, 33, 42, 43, 44, 45, 52